EXPLORING

decolonising themes in SA Sport History:

Issues and challenges

Francois Johannes Cleophas

Editor

SUN PRESS

Exploring decolonising themes in SA sport history: Issues and challenges

Published by AFRICAN SUN MeDIA under the SUN PReSS imprint

First edition 2018

ISBN 978-1-928357-94-0
ISBN 978-1-928357-95-7 (e-book)
https://doi.org/10.18820/9781928357957

Set in Gotham Book 8/11.5
Cover design, typesetting and production by AFRICAN SUN MeDIA

SUN PReSS is a licensed imprint of AFRICAN SUN MeDIA. Scholarly, professional and reference works are published under this imprint in print and electronic format.

This publication can be ordered directly from:
www.sun-e-shop.co.za
africansunmedia.snapplify.com (e-books)
www.africansunmedia.co.za

Contents

ACCOUNTS FROM THE COALFACE

Reflections on writing a post-colonial history of a colonial game

André Odendaal

Honorary Professor in History and Heritage Studies, University of the Western Cape

The great African novelist Chinua Achebe noted that 'in the colonial situation presence was the critical question, the crucial word. Its denial was the keynote of colonialist ideology' (Achebe 1992:346). The case of sport and sports history underlines his argument. In the four mainstream volumes of the history of South African cricket covering the years 1876–1960, only one scorecard appears relating to black cricketers, and they are entirely absent in the accompanying narratives about the game (Luckin 1915 and no date [1927], Duffus 1947, Bassano 1996). This gave rise to notions that black people did not play 'Western sports' like cricket and rugby. They were fixed into a caricatured past as 'primitive' people who somehow preferred hunting and dancing to these 'white man's games' (Archer & Boullion 1982:8–9). Apartheid and exclusion became naturalised eventually, even amongst those who were themselves subjugated. These assumptions about the 'naturalness' of the 'culture' of sport continue to be reproduced in new guises without any great self-awareness by a historically illiterate media and sports constituency in the democratic era, reproducing and making acceptable past exclusions in sport in the process.

South African sports history has in many ways come to resemble the much reviled school textbooks of the apartheid era which somehow managed to omit the names of Mandela, Sobukwe and Biko, the ANC, PAC and Sharpeville, from accounts of the political history of the country. No blood was 'spilled on these pages', one reviewer noted. They were 'history as negation', he observed. They were to the subject and education what the black hole is to matter: 'a kind of anti-knowledge'. This kind of history completely excluded black people as active agents in society. Only six black political figures, generally apartheid apologists, appear in one of the textbooks that ran to fifteen editions. This work became part of the broader pattern of colonial and apartheid control (Bundy 1977:69).

At the core of the project of decolonising South African sports history, therefore, is the effort to understand how the absences of the colonial subject in sport were engineered and how colonial narratives became fixed in the literature and minds of South Africans – and to attempt to redress this situation. We argue that this process of redress requires not so much band-aid patchwork on past (often shallowly empirical) narratives by adding some examples, in a changing context, to prove that black South Africans do indeed have

1

a sports history, but rather a full-scale re-imagining and rewriting of the history of sport in this country. This rewriting must inevitably go with painstaking research and readings in still under-exploited archives and fields of enquiry despite the pressures of the post-modern digital age to produce instant outcomes.

In pursuance of this goal, the writer has been project leader of a decades-long initiative to attempt to write the first post-colonial general history of a colonial game from inception to the present. This has resulted in the publication of *Cricket and Conquest* (Odendaal et al. 2016) and *Divided Country* (Odendaal et al. 2018), the first two volumes of a four-part series on *The History of South African Cricket Retold*, which seeks to retell the history of an entire sport in South Africa from day one in 1795 through 223 years to the present.

Rather than adapting or 'fiddling' with past colonial and apartheid narratives, this series seeks to fundamentally replace and supersede them. We have found that six main challenges await the post-colonial scholarly enterprise on South African sport. They are touched on here only in the briefest detail due to space constraints, but the above-mentioned volumes can be consulted for an elaboration of these themes.

1. *Putting in place new paradigms for understanding cricket's past*

    The first challenge, a priority for our project, was to put in place new paradigms for understanding cricket's past (and present) in South Africa by rooting the game in its social, economic, political and global context, and seeking to explain how mentalities and mindsets in sport were shaped over two centuries. In its founding myths, cricket was an innocent pastime played under sunny skies on the African veld in the spirit of fair play by quirky Englishmen and the few locals who understood its peculiarities and the delightfully eccentric nature of English culture (Murray & Vahed 2009:xv–xvi). We started by challenging the notion of cricket as a 'gentlemen's game' that has somehow been neutral, 'above politics' and marked by 'fair play' by demonstrating in detail how cricket arrived in Africa as part of the baggage of invading British military forces and how it spread step by step with them through the subcontinent in a hundred-year process of systematic and violent conquest. It was not by chance that King Williams Town won the first representative tournament in Africa for the Champion Bat in 1876 at a time when several thousand troops were stationed in that town shortly before the ninth 'frontier' war of dispossession. Or that that influential player and administrator William Milton was also cabinet secretary to Cecil John Rhodes and that he was one of six (out of the first ten) captains of the whites-only South African Cricket Association (SACA) who became leading colonial administrators in Rhodesia. One observer identified a cricket pad lying amongst the two thousand bodies and litter of battle at Isandlwana, and the legendary Hampshire, England and South African all-rounder Brigadier-General Robert Poore scored centuries and became Rhodesian tennis champion in between leading expeditions against the local inhabitants defending their land, which included the dynamiting of caves where people were seeking refuge (Murray & Vahed 2009:167–8).

    The inherent violence that underpinned cricket's growth in southern Africa, we argue, also shaped its character. The mindsets behind British and settler militarism directly incubated an exclusive 'culture' of cricket that became infused with notions of racism, narrow masculinity, Social Darwinism and imperial superiority, leading to the implementation of an official colour bar from 1894 onwards. It was impossible for the archetypal British game, with its close military associations, to remain innocent against the long background of conquest and dispossession. Indeed, there is ample evidence to show that it was tightly woven into the fabric of imperialism and colonial power in southern Africa (*Cricket and Conquest*, chapters 9, 24, 28, 29 and Epilogue).

The changing political economy after the discovery of diamonds and gold from the 1870s onward led to Britain consolidating its power over the whole of southern Africa, leading to the new Union of South Africa in 1910. Whereas initially there had been a promise of accommodating the political and sporting aspirations of an emerging black middle class within the developing colonial society, thereafter segregation became the key word. The 1913 Natives Land Act and the urban legislation of the 1920s and succeeding government policies set out systematically to control the movement, labour and living areas of black citizens. It was made clear to them that political rights and sport were for whites only. *Divided Country* shows how underlying tectonic shifts sausage-machined society into segregation until there were seven different 'national' cricket bodies existing at the same time in South Africa by the 1950s.

2. *Integrating, from the beginning, at every stage and in every area, the experiences of hitherto excluded black cricketers*

The second challenge in attempting a post-colonial cricket history was, logically, to go beyond existing colonial and apartheid narratives by integrating, from the beginning, at every stage and in every area, the experiences of hitherto excluded black cricketers in the country.

We have shown that colonised black players were incontestably among the pioneers of the game in South Africa and the broader colonial world in the nineteenth century, playing at a much earlier time and on a scale and at a level not yet appreciated (see, for example, *Cricket and Conquest*, chapters 3, 4, 11–12, 21–22, 25–27 and 33.) They took on white teams as early as the 1860s; started representative Native and later Malay Inter-Town Tournaments from 1884 onwards, which were amongst the earliest formal competitions in South African sport; launched inter-provincial competitions (for the Barnato Trophy) in the 1890s, the same decade that England's County Championship became official and Australia's Sheffield Shield and SACA's Currie Cup competitions were launched; and, they formed one of the earliest national controlling cricket bodies in the world in 1903, the South African Coloured Cricket Board (SACCB), which was only the third permanently established representative national association worldwide, preceding by two years the Australian Cricket Board and by a quarter of a century or more the West Indian, Indian, New Zealand and Pakistan cricket boards representative of the great Asian and Caribbean traditions of cricket.

We point out that the experiences of the eastern Cape 'school people' were comparable in certain ways with the Parsis from Mumbai, who were pioneers of cricket among the colonised people in India. Both communities acted as middlemen of sorts between the colonisers and the conquered native people, and developed strong cricket traditions. While the Parsis set up clubs earlier than the Africans, the latter played in inter-racial matches against British colonists earlier than the Indians. The southern Africans in addition preceded by some way the descendants of slaves and indentured workers on the islands of the Caribbean in setting up clubs and competitions (*Cricket and Conquest*, chapter 8). By the 1890s black cricketers proved themselves good enough to play international cricket, but Cecil John Rhodes and his cricket allies formally introduced sports segregation in 1894, barring them from playing in SACA's clubs, provincial competition and test matches, a ban that remained in place until the 1970s (*Cricket and Conquest*, chapters 26–27).

3

3. *Women out of a gender ghetto and into the mainstream of cricket history*

Thirdly, we argue, no new sport histories can avoid dealing with the issue of gender. Next to deep-seated race and class discrimination, ingrained sexism has been at the core of the 'traditions' and 'culture' of cricket since the start. For over a century the same power relations and socially constructed conventions that made cricket a white imperial game also reinforced patriarchal control over the female body, on and off the field. Cricket became so exclusionary in England and South Africa that the sexuality of those who sought to play it was questioned and turned into a source of ridicule. As scholars have shown, cricket was defined specifically as a 'gentlemen's game' as Empire-serving ideas of muscular Christianity became a feature of British public schools from the mid-nineteenth century. Women could play hockey, golf and tennis, but the famous WG Grace, conveying widely held stereotypes of the time, said women who played this game were 'neither ladies nor cricketers'. Therefore, this project also tries to take out of a gender ghetto, and insert into the mainstream of cricket history, the hitherto invisible role played by women in the socially constructed 'gentlemen's game'.

We show how women were present from the beginning in the game that reinforced patriarchal 'fair sex' and division of labour roles, at first as supporters, social accompaniments and providers of teas and lunches, but from the beginning of the twentieth century also as players. Influenced by British educational reformers, schools like Rodean, Pretoria Girls, Wynberg and Rustenberg introduced physical education and started school cricket teams. The first women's clubs appeared on the margins of men's clubs with heavy British cultures such as the Wanderers in Johannesburg and Ramblers in Bloemfontein. Among them were women's rights activists such as Winifred Kingswell. Like their male counterparts, black women emerging from the eastern Cape mission schools too became keen followers of this British game from the 1880s onwards. (For details see *Cricket and Conquest*, introduction and chapters 31–32 and *Divided Country*, introduction and chapters 18–19 and 32.)

The extension of the franchise to women in Britain and other countries after World War 1 led directly to organised cricket, national bodies and the beginnings of women's international cricket in the late 1920s and 1930s. Political power enabled women to exercise greater choices and options in the social sphere too. South Africa lagged behind until the whites-only South Africa and Rhodesia Women's Cricket Association (SARWCA) was formed in 1952 and this led to annual inter-provincial cricket weeks for the Simons Trophy and the first South African team and test matches in 1960. Laws, customs, fashions and ideas of 'femininity' constantly intersected with the way the game was played and supported. The mere act of playing was subversive in itself but at the same time (politically conservative) women cricketers continued to romanticise the protocols of cricket and its conservative, classist, racist and patriarchal culture. But a strong strand of feminism was evident as well and women cricketers set about in a determined way to open up a niche for themselves on the fringes of the game, a move that after many decades led to their full acceptance as cricketers, together with men, by Cricket South Africa and the International Cricket Council from 2005 onwards (Gupta 2013).

4. *Reconstituting the entire statistical history of South African cricket*

Given the depth of past exclusions and the fact that statistics are integral to the culture and romance of cricket, *Cricket and Conquest* and the companion volumes, fourthly, start the process of reconstituting the entire statistical history of South African cricket.

This has been one of the most painstaking and satisfying searching-for-a-needle-in-a-haystack challenges in the project. Statistics do not make for glamorous narratives, and they too are admittedly subjectively or socially constructed, but they are indispensable in the attempt to make visible in professional, standardised ways the extent and depth of organisation and involvement of those excluded in the past. Researchers should not assume that the evidence does not exist because it is not staring at you in the face. The richness of the statistical chapters in the two works is the result largely of the treasure house of material uncovered in the vernacular pages of the early independent black press from the 1880s onwards. Here the origins of the sport and the political mobilisation of the early African intellectuals and activists have been recorded in their own hand. This reconstituting of the record needs the full attention of readers and can be engaged with in depth in the introduction and chapters 15 and 34–35 of *Cricket and Conquest* and the introduction and chapters 25–32 of *Divided Country*. Our books fundamentally challenge the colonial records of cricket worldwide. The end result is that from one scorecard in four volumes of mainstream colonial/apartheid history covering the 84-year period from 1876 to 1960 we now have records for 80 representative tournaments involving over 500 provincial and national matches and some 2, 3000 black and women players for that period. And Volume 4, exclusively statistical, will deal with exclusions since 1960. In this way, thousands of invisible players from the past, become identifiable living, rounded cricketers, with particular pedigrees and backgrounds. More than 60 pre-1960 provincial and national team photographs complete this picture of cricket wholeness, destroying any credibility current official South African cricket records, which have reproduced colonial and apartheid apartheid-era history unfiltered, might still have.

5. *Contextualised organisational histories for all eleven national cricket bodies in South Africa, 1890 to the present*

The fifth goal of this series is to provide for the first time standardised organisational histories for each of the 11 national cricket boards that have existed in the ethno-religious chessboard that was South African cricket between 1890 and the present, namely the SACA, SACCB, SAICCB, SABCB, SAICU, SACBOC, SARWCA, SACU, SACB, SAWCA and the UCBSA, renamed Cricket South Africa (CSA) in 2005. Again, most of these national bodies are scarcely known about today and half of them have had no formal history until now. The series attempts to provide for each:

- the reasons for their emergence and how they were formed;
- who their administrators, top players and champion teams were;
- a historical overview of their development;
- statistics of the main competitions and tournaments each board ran;
- a comprehensive list of the national and provincial players of each; and
- details about the matches played by the various 'national' teams.

At one stage seven of these 11 bodies existed at the same time, all with their own national structures and leadership, all organising their own club leagues and provincial tournaments (in the same cities and towns) and all selecting specific South African teams. This dizzying array of acronyms was ultimately part of a single story. Rather than dealing with these bodies as 'own affairs' matters in disconnected silos or ghettoes, the authors try to weave them into a single narrative full of overlap, disunion, misalignment and discordance as the population was increasingly categorised and segregated on racial lines in an institutionally violent society.

Black and women cricketers organised into these national bodies were active participants in the unfolding history of the game in South Africa from the start. Looking back in retrospect, their early vision had a defining long-term impact on South African cricket. For example, the new SACCB declared in clause 25 of its founding constitution in 1903 that 'this Board does not recognise any distinction amongst the various sporting peoples of South Africa, whether by Creed, Nationality or otherwise' (KZNCU Archives). It became the first repository of a vision of unity in cricket across class and colour divides that would be finally realised when democracy arrived in the last decade of that century.

6. *Beyond master narratives and binaries: Looking for new ways of narrating the past*

The sixth and final point we wish to make is that while this series is in many respects a group biography about cricket structures and formal organising against the backdrop of institutionalised discrimination in a segregated colonial society, we hope this series also goes beyond old sporting binaries – good/bad, apartheid/struggle, men/women, insiders/outsiders – to reveal something of the vibrancy, creativity, contradictions, joy and feelings which accompanied the playing of cricket in many different communities over many years: from the dreams and aspirations of individuals to the rich creativity and social tapestry found in team and club dynamics, to the determination and balletic skills of those who made it to the top.

We hope the series encourages deeper historical understandings by promoting multi-perspectival approaches that explore and question rather than fix in simple terms the complex dynamics involved in the playing and organising of sport over the past two centuries. The book also seeks to give insights into changing identities and the mindsets and motivations that were at play in different cricket constituencies in the country and multi-dimensional cricket environment over the past 223 years. By 1890, several different cricket traditions, each located within a specific context and social milieu, became evident in southern Africa. At various times, particular individuals and cricket communities had different views of themselves and different visions for the future. Exploring cricket's intricate origins and the way in which the different strands of the game evolved thus also helps illuminate changing notions of identity in South Africa over the past 200 years, contributing to better understanding of current debates and struggles. See, for example, *Cricket and Conquest*, chapters 20–26. There were no fixed binaries, and cricketers had overlapping identities, which created the possibility at one stage of the colonised people being accepted into the colonial cricket mainstream before the twentieth century brought fragmentation on a scale not experienced in any other cricketing nation. One of the goals of the book is to explore the complexities and contradictions that went with the growth of the game in this country and we have found new scholarship about how historical knowledge is produced and the different ways of telling and deconstructing narratives very useful.

Conclusion

In a review of *Cricket and Conquest*, the journalist Michael Morris concluded that the book's details exposed not so much a loss of memory as 'erasure' and 'a staggering delusion' (Morris 2016). The repression of cricket memories in South Africa came about not as an accident of history, but as a direct consequence of it. Therefore, as mentioned, rather than adapting or tampering with past colonial and apartheid narratives, this series seeks to fundamentally replace and supersede them. We hope there is some truth in Prof Ashwin Desai's comments that *Cricket and Conquest* 'bowls over prevailing histories, de-colonising existing narratives of the game in a manner that does not seek to consolidate an innings, but opens up the field of study ... throwing all that came before into a spin [and ensuring] that what was will never be the same' (Desai, Readers' report, quoted in Odendaal et al. 2016).

The brand-new accounts and records provided here will, we trust, help undermine destructive and deeply ingrained patriarchal, colonial and apartheid mindsets which have been used as self-righteous excuses to exclude and discriminate against people in real life – right up to the present day. The goal is that they provide a platform for new research areas, insights and interpretations and contribute in small ways to making South African cricket and sport in general genuinely inclusive and actively intolerant of the inherited brand of class snobbishness, racism, sexism and social discrimination that has for so long been integral to its culture.

We believe that it is necessary to start talking about the history of South African cricket and sport in decisively different ways in the future. Writing these types of histories opens windows for scholars to understand broader social issues in society and will help both researchers and readers go forward armed with clearer understandings of the power relations and complex dynamics that have shaped South Africa's history. As Brailsford pointed out that, 'Ever since human beings began to live in organised communities, politics and play have been irresistibly entangled' (Brailsford 1991:45). And, we should be mindful too of the reminder by the geographer Harold Wesso that all 'geographical space', including that used for the playing and administration of cricket, 'is socially produced' (Wesso 1994:332).

Acknowledgements

Thank you to my co-authors Christopher Merrett, Krish Reddy and Jonty Winch for their contributions and insights which are included in this paper, Dr Francois Cleophas for the invitation to participate in this project, and Zohra Ebrahim and Tony Tabatznik for their generosity and support.

References

Achebe, C. 1992. 'African literatures as celebration', *Dissent,* Summer 1992.

Archer, R. & Boullion, A. 1982. *The South African Game: Sport and racism.* Zed Press, London.

Bassano, B. 1996. *South African Cricket, Vol. IV, 1947–1960.* Cricket Connections International, Turner's Hill, UK.

Brailsford, D. 1991. *Sport, Time and Society: The British at play.* London.

Bundy, C. 1977. *Re-making the past. New perspectives on South African history.* UCT summer school lectures, Cape Town.

Duffus, L. 1947. *South African Cricket 1927–1947.* South African Cricket Association, Johannesburg.

Gupta, R. 2013. 'Bowled out of the game: Nationalism and gender equality in Indian cricket'. *Berkeley Journal of Entertainment and Sports Law* 2(1).

KZNCU Archives: Krish Reddy Collection, Durban District Indian Cricket Union report/ meetings, 1912/13. SA Coloured Cricket Board – rules etc.

Luckin, M.W. 1915. *The History of South African Cricket, including the scores of all important matches since 1878.* Johannesburg, WJ Horton.

Luckin, M.W. no date. *South African Cricket, 1917–1927: A complete record of all first-class cricket in South Africa since the war.* Published by the author, Johannesburg.

Morris, M. 2016. 'Uncovering SA cricket's hidden history, An exercise to tell the non-racial history of South African cricket reveals a staggering delusion'. *Weekend Argus*, 19 November 2016.

Murray, B. & Vahed, G. (eds.). 2009. *Empire and Cricket: The South African experience 1884–1914.* Unisa Press, Pretoria.

Odendaal, A., Reddy, K., Merrett, C. & Winch, J. 2016. *Cricket and Conquest, The history of South African cricket retold, volume 1, 1795–1914.* BestRed in association with Cricket South Africa and the Human Sciences Research Council, Cape Town.

Odendaal, A., Reddy, K. & Merrett, C. 2018. *Divided Country, The history of South African cricket retold, volume 2, 1915–1950s.* BestRed in association with Cricket South Africa and the Human Sciences Research Council, Cape Town.

Wesso, H.M. 1994. 'The colonization of geographic thought: The South African experience' in A. Godlewska and N. Smith (eds.). *Geography and Empire.* OUP, Oxford.

From the editor

Francois Cleophas

Senior Lecturer in Sport History, Department of Sport Science, Stellenbosch University

This publication includes the articulations of academic researchers, professionals and retired sportspeople who were requested to explore their unique areas of interest in sport. They place themselves at the centre of discourses that dispel myths that blacks had no sport significance prior to 1994. In effect, they confirm the idea that blacks became the victims of a colonial violence that reduced them to nothingness (Snyman, 2015:268). In a sense the contributors challenge this spirit of the past where there was only one narrative – a white male sport tradition. They can do so because they all have first-hand experience of the topic they articulate. The contributors of the various chapters are thus purposeful in their foregrounding of a narrative hitherto unexplored or given scant consideration. This is part of the decolonisation process of rediscovery and recovery. In quoting Chilisa (2012), Le Grange defines rediscovery and recovery as processes whereby colonised peoples rediscover and recover their own history, culture, language and identity (Le Grange 2016:3). Decolonisation in sport, as elsewhere, concerns itself with discarding what has been "wrongly written and interrogating distortions of people's life experiences, negative labelling, deficit theorizing, culturally deficient models that pathologized the colonised … and retelling the stories of the past and envisioning the future" (Le Grange 2016:3).

André Odendaal remarked at a recent gathering that: "Decolonising the history of sport is part of a broader intellectual project". This project, according to Grosfoguel, quoted in Snyman (2015:267) is one that aims to "epistemologically transcend and decolonize the Western canon". This publication does this by intentionally avoiding the creation of a new hierarchy: one which dismisses the voices from "below". A concerted effort was made to create a degree of inclusivity that bridges the span between the historical actors and those who write about them. In this way the "silences" in coverages left by orthodox history practices up till now are starting to fill up. This is achieved by accounts in Section A that are dedicated to academic writing whilst Section B is reserved for the voices of those who occupied spaces defined by issues and challenges in South African sport history.

Oppressed voices are articulated in a manner that does not necessarily dovetail with Western epistemology. Farieda Khan's account of the Cape Province Mountain Club is an example of creating new South African sport narratives from outside the official archives. Khan highlights the nuances in the sport colour bar where blacks, whilst being at the receiving end of white racism, initially assimilated racist colonial attitudes in the Cape Province Mountain Club before radical shifts were made in the wake of the 1976 Soweto riots. Ultimately, Khan brings to the fore the political potency of black recreation that was silenced by colonial and apartheid-era historians. Similarly, Francois Cleophas surfaces new information in the chapter, 'Black Athletics in Cape Town prior to 1920'. This narrative on black provincial athletic history was previously, and continues to be, under-represented in South African history. It shows how the participation in organised athletics was linked to limited opportunities of 'leadership' available to persons of colour. It also shows how the local is shaped by aspirations located within the global – hence "the early organisation of athletics in Cape Town's Coloured community internalised and promoted British values". In the process, Western epistemology is taken to task for the marks it left and is still leaving in its wake, in terms of the power relations it created and sustains (Snyman 2015:269).

This publication, unapologetically, aims at creating cultural treasures out of communities that were socially and politically sidelined during periods of colonialism and apartheid. These cultural treasures emerge out of records created by historians, of whom many are guilty of ignoring or downplaying subterranean forces in black sport traditions. Gustav Venter's chapter on football serves to highlight some of these subterranean forces at play within the non-racial sport movement. Venter highlights what he sees as "the incompatibility between ideology and practicality as far as professional football in apartheid South Africa was concerned".

There is also an awareness amongst scholars engaging decolonisation themes that the manner in which history is created also needs to be interrogated. The purpose of these cross conversations is thus a deliberate attempt to avoid the historian growing above the events that are being articulated. A further need for these cross conversations is to avoid creating new mythologies based on untruths. These mythologies arise out of a need for the creation of faultless people that ironically reflect an extension of a colonised narrative. It could be argued that the decolonial turn affirms the possibility of different epistemic foundations on the basis of a very particular geo- and body-politics of knowledge within the realm of those excluded because of the hegemony of the Western paradigm (Snyman 2015:269). Snyders reinterprets the Coloured character, Gamat Behardien, as a person of his time, in a response to previous work that denigrated him as 'subservient jester'. Behardien is presented as a full person who occupies a space defined by the intersection of international sport, national politics and individual aspirations in a society where the opportunities were few. This chapter broadens the lens with which future historians can view complexities and entanglements that surround characters labelled, 'sell-outs', 'Uncle Toms' and 'quislings'. This approach places this publication at a 'decolonial turn' where "critical ways of exploring black complicity in colonial and apartheid projects" are approached. It also juxtaposes the re-constructed view of Gamat as a full historical character with the two-dimensional account where the same character is defined by the function he serves in a particular time and place: as mascot. By linking so-called minor sport codes (athletics, baseball, physical education, mountaineering) and activities at grassroots level, this publication places national decolonisation discourses within community affairs. Snyders makes this link in his second article, "The sound of the hickory and the roar of the crowds", between local developments and international diplomacy in his reflections on South African baseball history. This was an attempt to foreground the role of baseball in the colonisation of South Africa that revealed its complicity in exclusionary and racial practices.

The chapter entitled 'Muslim women and sport: On traversing the politics of "religious" identity' by Nuraan Davids challenges constructed Western gazes by changing the location of the viewer. Davids constructs a lens that reveals the limitations of Western gazes on

Muslim women in sport and creates the space within which to reconsider previous certainties that accompanied such uncritical gazes.

In certain cases, such as Sigi Howes' description of physical education, an attempt is made to place local stories, in greater need of decolonising perspectives, in national and international perspective. Here Howes explores how a colonial narrative "links incidents and people who, on the surface, appear to be unrelated but are often interrelated". André Alexander reflects on a career in non-racial school athletics, soccer and baseball on the Cape Flats during the 1980s and how this shaped life views in the 21st century. Similarly, Andrew September recalls his involvement in non-racial athletics, gymnastics, physical education and roller skating at community level that led to a lifelong involvement in sport. Shaun Vester pens down his achievements as a non-racial athlete who recorded international times under extreme harsh social and economic circumstances. A common thread running through these accounts is a struggle against adversity while "being angry but not bitter" at being denied opportunities for participation. This may be best understood by Robin April's reflection, as an aspect of an athletic president's life story, that although "we lived and worked in trying times, athletics gave us lots of joy and very good memories". This is so because local non-racial sport comes out of a tradition of organisation with a historical legacy that transcends a victimhood mentality. William Pick adds another dimension of the importance of local histories in decolonising sport discourses. He argues in his chapter that the history of a local cricket union can reveal a process of transformation from a British colonial gentlemen's game to a rallying point of progressive forces in a society striving for political rights and social equity. It is this historical process that mimics the experience of so many colonised populations all over the world. On the issue of new epistemologies, Dewald Steyn's chapter reveals resilience to the decolonised narrative that is still present in current discourses in South African sport. Steyn's search for records in the archives (private and official) of the non-racial South African Amateur Athletic Board, as a means of writing that particular narrative, proves this point. Despite sincere attempts to record non-racial sport history, an over-dependence on archival sources for creating narratives in this area is futile. This is so because "the archive has lost its sole authority on the design of the past" (Lalu 2008:158).

The narratives contained in this volume may be described as a contribution towards a decolonisation discourse in South African sport studies, started by historians such as André Odendaal, Albert Grundlingh and others. The specific accounts in this book however are early conversations and reflections on hidden South African sport histories. Many of the accounts contained in this publication eminate from unofficial records and can be regarded as a start of a history, or a first narrative, for others to extend. After all, no historical account can be so arrogant as to declare a historical completeness in one lifetime.

In summary, this book grappled with the question posed by Morgan Ndlovo: What should a decolonised South African (sport) history be? Ndlovo answered: "A decolonised South African (sport) history will ideally consist of ecologies of different historical narratives that do not assume any pretence to objectivity and universality" (Ndlovo 2013: 10). In conclusion therefore, this publication affords the sceptic future historian the opportunity to revisit traces and accounts to determine their veracity in order to further explore issues and challenges in the decolonisation debate in South African sport history.

References

Lalu, P. 2008. Recalling community, refiguring archive. In: B. Bennet, C. Julius & C. Soudien (eds). *City. Site. Museum. Reviewing memory practices at the District Six Museum.* Cape Town: District Six Museum. 158–165.

Le Grange, L. 2016. Decolonising the university curriculum. *South African Journal of Higher Education*, 30(2):1-12.

Ndlovo, M. 2013. Mobilising History for nation-building in South Africa: A decolonial perspective. *Yesterday & Today*, July, 9:1-12.

Snyman, G. 2015. Responding to the decolonial turn: Epistemic Vulnerability. *Missionalia*, 43(3):266-291.

Acknowledgements

The editor expresses thanks to the following people and institutions for assistance in various ways:

- ▾ Prof Eugene Cloete
- ▾ Prof Yusuf Waghid
- ▾ Mr Bongani Mgijima
- ▾ Prof André Odendaal
- ▾ Ms Michelle Heswick
- ▾ Mr Clement du Plessis
- ▾ Mr Dean Matthews
- ▾ Stellenbosch University Sport Science Department

This publication is in memory of two people –
Mona Cleophas (née Small) and Ron Eland.

Mona Small
Source: Francois Cleophas, private collection

THE 1948 OLYMPIC GAMES BRITISH WEIGHT-LIFTING TEAM
Alf Knight; 2, Oscar State (Team Manager); 3, Bill Watson; 4, Julian Creus; 5, Jim Halliday (Team Captain); 6, W. A. Pullum (Team Coach); 7, Ernie Pepplatt; 8, Ernie Roe; 9, Syd Kemble; 10, Mel Barnett; 11, Ron Eland; 12, Denis Hallett. (Figures run from left to right, 1 to 10 standing, 11 and 12 seated.)
(From an oil painting by Noel Syers)

Olympic Team
Source: Halliday, J. *Olympic Weight-Lifting With Body-Building For All* (London: Pullum, 1950)

Decolonising sport:
Some thoughts

Lesley Le Grange

Distinguished Professor, Department of Curriculum Studies, Stellenbosch University

Introduction

South African student protests, which took place in 2015 and 2016, have been the impetus for a renewed interest in decolonisation or decoloniality (Le Grange 2016), not only in the realm of education, but also in other spheres of social life such as sport. Interest in the decolonisation of sport in South Africa is evidenced by an inaugural conference that explored decolonisation of sport, held on 17 and 18 September 2017. The conference was hosted by the Department of Sport Science at Stellenbosch University (SU) together with the SU Museum and brought together academics and former athletes and administrators to share experiences, and to deliberate on the topic of decolonising sport. Narratives shared by individuals and some of the deliberations of the conference are captured in this book.

Not much has been written on the decolonisation of sport, both internationally and in South Africa. However, some seminal works/moments are worth mentioning. Combeau-Mari (2011) argues that *The Community Games of April 1960* was an important decolonising moment in sport. Combeau-Mari also describes how political astuteness, sport, the political rhetoric of fraternity and an all-powerful colonial presence intersected to produce a decolonising/decolonial moment. The Community Games of 1960, which was held in Antananarivo, was based on the model of the Olympic Games and brought together all French-speaking African nations and French overseas departments and territories. The context of these games was the liberalisation of the French Union by General de Gaulle upon recognising the frailty of the colonial system introduced by the Fourth Republic of France (Combeau-Mari 2011). The upshot of this was a new structure called Community (Communauté), which entitled colonies to self-determine the status that they wished to adopt vis-à-vis France. Combeau-Mari (2011) avers that the Community Games presented an unexpected opportunity for the French government to retain friendly ties and to harness future relations with African nations into possible cooperation. At the onset of the games, it was obvious that French athletes were advantaged by years of training, superior infrastructure and facilities. Yet, as the games unfolded, the headlines in the French press focused on how athletes from mainland France triumphed at the games. The games became a decolonial moment when

15

French superiority was met with annoyance and anti-colonial umbrage. As Combeau-Mari (2011, p. 1722) cogently puts it:

> ... France intended to remind its former partners that it remained a power that could not be ignored. In the framework of decolonization, this form of arrogance had become intolerable. The sporting event became a platform for the expression of frustration and anti-colonial resentment.

Closer to home, in post-apartheid South Africa we have seen texts produced, which document the history of black sport in the country. I shall mention just a few. In his book *Forgotten Heroes – History of Black Rugby 1882–1992*, Booley (1998) documents a 100-year history of black rugby in South Africa. Similarly a black history of cricket has been retold so as to decentre mainstream white-only cricket history. Two of the key works produced in this regard are: *The story of an African game* by Odendaal (2003) and *Cricket and conquest* by Odendaal, Reddy, Merrett and Winch (2016). In the context of school sport, the history of non-racial athletics has also been documented in recent years (see for example Cleophas & Van der Merwe, 2009a, 2009b, Cleophas, 2014). All of the works mentioned are decolonial ones, and I shall elaborate on this later in the chapter. However, decolonisation/decoloniality in relation to sport should not only involve the retelling of sport histories, which colonised peoples enaged with/in as excercises in mimicry. Mimicry is a term that has been produced in the field of postcolonial studies to describe the ambivalent relationship between coloniser and colonised, whereby the colonised subject 'mimics' the coloniser:,"by adopting the coloniser's cultural habits, assumptions, institutions and values, the result is never a simple reproduction of those traits" (Ashcroft, Griffiths & Tiffin, 2003) – in this instance the mimicking of sport codes played by the coloniser. What makes the relationship between coloniser and colonised ambivalent is the potential for the colonised to redefine this relationship. For example, we have seen how West Indian cricket came to redefine fast-bowling and how they dominated cricket in the late 1970s and 1980s. In the field of athletics we have, for example, witnessed African athletes, since the post World War II era, dominate middle- and long-distance running and athletes of African descent dominate sprint events.

More than retelling the history of what has become mainstream sport, decolonising of sport should also involve the (re)discovering of indigenous sports/games. In the context of educational research Wagner (1993) distinguishes between the constructs *blank spots* and *blind spots*. For him, *blank spots* are what scientists know enough about to question but do not answer, and *blind spots* are what they don't know enough about or care about. Wagner's constructs could have relevance to our discussion. The history of black participation in sport codes such as soccer, cricket and rugby were *blank spots* during the colonial period (and I include the apartheid era) but has become mainstreamed in post-apartheid South Africa, which could have potentially transformative effects on these sport codes. Indigenous sports/games were blind spots during the colonial period, and largely remain so in post-apartheid South Africa.

In this chapter, I shall discuss what is meant by decolonisation/decoloniality, and suggest how sport in South Africa is being decolonised and what might be done to advance efforts to decolonise sport. I end with some parting thoughts.

What is decolonisation/decoloniality?

Put simply, decolonisation is the undoing of colonisation. First-generation colonialism was the conquering of the physical spaces and bodies of the colonised, and second-generation colonialism was the colonisation of people's minds through disciplines such as education, science, economics, sport and law. Neo-colonialism was coined by the first President of independent Ghana, Kwame Nkrumah. It relates to the achievement of technical independence by a country, but which is still under the influence of ex-colonial or newly developed superpowers. Such superpowers could be international monetary bodies, multinational corporations, cartels as well as education and cultural institutions (Ashcroft, Griffiths & Triffin, 2003). In the context of our discussion, we can add international institutions/bodies such a Fédération Internationale de Natation Amateur (FINA), Fédération Internationale Football Association (FIFA), World Rugby (WR), and so forth. Nkrumah argued that neo-colonialism is a more insidious form of colonialism because it is more difficult to detect (Ashcroft et al. 2003).

Chilisa (2012) suggests five phases in the process of decolonisation: *rediscovery and recovery, mourning*; *dreaming*; *commitment* and *action*. Rediscovery and recovery is the process whereby colonised peoples rediscover and recover their own history, culture, language and identity. Mourning refers to the process of lamenting the continued assault on the world's colonised/oppressed peoples' identities and social realities. It is an important part of healing and leads to dreaming. Dreaming is when colonised peoples invoke their histories, worldviews and indigenous knowledge systems to theorise and imagine alternative possibilities – in this instance a more inclusive future for sport. Smith (1999) identified the following elements of decolonisation: *deconstruction and reconstruction*; *self-determination and social justice*; *ethics*; *language*; *internationalisation of indigenous experiences; history*; and *critique*. Deconstruction and reconstruction concern discarding what has been wrongly written, and "interrogating distortions of people's life experiences, negative labelling, deficit theorizing, genetically deficient or culturally deficient models that pathologized the colonised … and retelling the stories of the past and envisioning the future" (Chilisa 2012:17). Self-determination and social justice relates to the struggle by those who have been marginalised by the Western academy and is about seeking legitimacy for knowledge that is embedded in their own histories, experiences and ways of viewing reality. Ethics relates to the formulation, legislation and dissemination of ethical issues related to the protection of indigenous knowledge systems. Language concerns the importance of teaching/learning in indigenous languages as part of the anti-imperialist struggle. Internationalisation of indigenous experiences relates to international scholars sharing common experiences, issues and struggles of colonised peoples in global and local spaces. History, in this instance, involves a study of the past to recover the history, culture and languages of colonised peoples and to use it to inform the present. Critique concerns a critical appraisal of the imperial model of the academy that "continues to deny the colonised and historically marginalised other space to communicate from their own frames of reference" (Chilisa 2012:19). Some of the dimensions of decolonisation mentioned are relevant to sport, a discussion that is explored further in the next section of the chapter. But, it would be apposite at this juncture to first briefly discuss what is meant by decoloniality.

Decoloniality is a construct that has been produced by a group of Latin American scholars, and is a critique or an analytic of coloniality. The work of these scholars mainly focuses on the "coloniality of knowledge" and the "coloniality of being" (see Mignolo 2007:156–157). These scholarly deliberations are complex and I shall not explore them in detail here; suffice to provide some broad understanding of coloniality/decoloniality so that we can apply them in some way to sport. Decolonial scholars argue that although former European colonies attained independence and, in this sense, we live in postcolonial times, the logic of coloniality remains with us. In other words, the systems of power that classify (othering), denigrate and subjugate remain prevalent, and in a contemporary globalising world are more insidious than previous more naked forms of colonisation. Quijano (2007) describes the colonial matrix of power as having four interlocking domains: control of economy (land appropriation, exploitation of labour, control of natural resources); control of authority (institution, army); control of gender and sexuality (family, education) and control of subjectivity and knowledge (epistemology, education and identity formation). In relation to sport, decoloniality could involve asking critical questions such as: who controls the economy of sport internationally and in South Africa (including who owns sport infrastructure and facilities); who controls the institutions/organisations of sport; who produces sports knowledge (including its histories); how are identities (per)formed or constructed through/in discourses on sport? Decoloniality therefore concerns a critical awareness of the logic of coloniality (the colonial matrix of power), is a critique of coloniality, resists expressions of coloniality and takes actions to overcome coloniality. Applied to South Africa, the coloniality/decoloniality lens enables one to understand that apartheid was a particular manifestation of coloniality rather than a period distinct from colonialism, as Jansen (2017) suggests.

On decolonising sport in South Africa

The published works on (re)telling histories of black/non-racial sport in South Africa and those mentioned in this book are decolonial ones because they are critiques of the colonial matrix of power that Mignolo (2007) and Quijano (2007) articulate. What (re)telling South African black sport histories do is to de-centre a white history of sport and by so doing engenders transformative effects on the future of sport for all South Africa because it serves as a basis for imagining sport differently. The narratives and deliberations shared in this book also resonate with the phases or dimensions of decolonisation that Chilisa (2012) and Smith (1999) write about. The stories told are about the rediscovery and recovery of the authors' own histories and the collective history of black sport in South Africa. The narratives are also about deconstructing a white-only history of sport in South Africa, by discarding the negative labelling and deficit ways in which black sport persons have been framed. Moreover, it presents opportunities for reconstructing the history of sport in South Africa, as well as individual and collective identities. Perhaps Chilisa's mourning does not feature strongly in this book and requires some consideration in future projects. In post-apartheid South Africa blacks are often told by whites to move on, to forget about apartheid. But, mourning is an important ingredient in the healing process and a necessary step of decolonisation. The pain of historical exclusion in sport needs to be shared and felt – we have not had a Truth & Reconciliation process in Sport in South Africa as Francois Cleophas mentioned at a 'Reflection on the 1995 World Cup' symposium at the Stellenbosch University Museum in 2015. The idea that sport unifies, as the euphoria which accompanied events such as the 1995 Rugby World Cup and South Africa's recent victory in a rugby test against England (under the leadership of a first black captain) suggests, is a fiction. Such blissful moments hide the racial tensions and divisions prevalent in South African society, which a recent sport incident layed bare – the Willemse-Mallett-Botha affair that played itself out in a Super Sport studio and beyond. On its own sport cannot be a unifying factor whilst the colonial matrix of power remains entrenched – both in broader South African society and in sport codes such as rugby. Decoloniality requires asking critical questions such as who, for example, controls the institutions of rugby and who owns/controls the media houses that are the dominant broadcasters of rugby in South Africa?

Quijano's (2007) domain of the colonial matrix of power, the control of gender and sexuality, is worth some attention. The contributions of women at the decolonisation of sport conference as well as to this book are encouraging as are the experiences of some of the most marginalised women in sport – Muslim women – leaving us with much to reflect upon. But, the contributions at the conference and to this book were/are dominated by men, which is indicative of how all sport, including black sport, has been male-dominated in practice. As is the case with society broadly, in sport, women are marginalised in all kinds of ways: professional sportswomen's earnings are less, women's sport codes receive less sponsorship revenue, their sport codes receive less television coverage, and so forth. But, it is incidences such as Danny Jordaan's unopposed re-election as South African Football Association (SAFA) president, despite being accused of raping a woman (and I not suggesting that he is guilty) that is particularly telling about the marginalised positions of women in South African society. Addressing the issue of gender equity in sport is a crucial dimension of decolonising of sport.

But, there is another matter that is crucial to decolonising sport and links to Smith's (1999) dimensions: self-determination and social justice and the internationalisation of indigenous experiences. I refer here to the need to give greater prominence to indigenous sports/games and their internationalisation. In different parts of the world we are witnessing efforts to promote indigenous sports/games. In the summer of 2009 three organisations in Canada signed a historic agreement to form the Indigenous Sport, Physical Activity & Recreation Council, pledging to work together to promote Indigenous sport. They developed a detailed strategy, the Aboriginal Sport, Recreation and Physical Activity Strategy (ASRPA), comprising guiding principles in the form of five pillars, each having core priorities and actions. Also in Canada, the Manitoba Aboriginal Sports and Recreational Council Incorporated (MASRC) was established in 1988 and incorporated in 1994. Through the MASRC, the indigenous people of Manitoba participate annually in the North American Indigenous Games (NAIG). In 2017 the following sports were included in the NAIG held in Toronto: 3-D Archery, Athletics, Badminton, Baseball, Basketball, Canoe/Kayak, Golf, Lacrosse, Rifle shooting, Soccer, Softball, Swimming, Wrestling and Volleyball (http://www.masrc.com/maig_2017). Lacrosse, (a game played with sticks and a ball) would be familiar to some South African readers. Snyders (2016) documents the origins and early development of Lacrosse in Natal, South Africa. Although, now codified and played in different parts of the world, Lacrosse is part of the cultural tradition of the *Iroquois* people inhabiting what is now New York and Pennsylvania. The game may have developed as early as 1100 CE among indigenous peoples of Turtle Island in North America (see Liss, 1970).

In South Africa, there is evidence that a South African Sports Commission on Indigenous Sports was established and had a meeting in 2002 (https://pmg.org.za/committee-meeting/1403/). It is uncertain as to what the outcome of this Commission's work was. However, in 2017 a second Indigenous Games event was held at the Sandton Convention Centre so as to promote South African cultural values (http://www.sascoc.co.za/2017/04/21/indigenous-games-to-be-showcased-at-arnold-classic-africa/). The event brought together participants from all provinces and seven Indigenous games disciplines were included: Kjati (rope skipping game), Diketo (stone grabbing and throwing game), Dibeke (running ball game), Ntonga (stick fighting game), Drie Stokkies (games played with three sticks) and two board games, Ncuva and Moraborba (board games resembling chess or checkers). Part of decolonising sport must be giving prominence to Indigenous games which, embedded in South African cultural traditions, has connections to particular places and peoples' identities. This is different to problematic identities that mainstream sport produces such as what soccer does in a country like Brazil. Brazilian soccer gives all its inhabitants a sense that they are all Brazilian – when the Brazilian soccer team plays, citizens are all Brazilian. But this Brazilian identity that soccer produces hides the gross inequalities in the country and the tensions/divisions based on race and class. Another way in which Indigenous sports/games could gain prominence is through their internationalisation whereby indigenous people get together to share common experiences through participating in sports/games.

Some parting thoughts

In this chapter I have discussed what decolonisation/decoloniality means and explored some of its implications for sport. I pointed out that contributions to this book and other published works, which retell histories of black/non-racial sport in South Africa, are efforts in decolonialty. I noted some of the blank spots and blind spots in the history of sport (both black and white) such as gender and sexuality and the inclusion of Indigenous games. Addressing these shortcomings is important in advancing the decolonising of sport in South Africa. The inaugural conference held at Stellenbosch University in 2017 and the contributions to this book make important contributions to the project/process of decolonising sport in South Africa.

On a personal level, reading the chapters brought back memories of supporting non-racial sport for many years. I personally witnessed the remarkable athletic achievements (against the odds) of many of the contributors to this book and one of them, Andrew September, attended the same school, Heathfield High School, that I did. The personal narratives of the former athletes remind me of our decolonial 'disobedience' not to 'play normal sport in an abnormal society' during apartheid.

I do not wish to conclude by summarising things for the reader, but hope that I have managed to open up some ideas of how we might advance the project of decolonising sport in South Africa.

References

Ashcroft, B., Griffiths, G. & Tiffin, H. 2003. *Post-colonial studies: Key concepts*. London and New York: Routledge.

Booley, A. 1998. *Forgotten heroes – History of Black rugby 1882-1992*. Cape Town: Manie Booley Publications.

Chilisa, B. 2012. *Indigenous research methodologies*. Los Angeles: Sage Publications.

Cleophas, F.J. & Van der Merwe, F.J.G. 2009a. Physical Education and Physical Culture in the Coloured community of the Western Cape, 1837-1966. A literature review. *African Journal for Physical, Health Education, Recreation and Dance*, 15(1):102-121.

Cleophas, F.J. & Van der Merwe, F.J.G. 2009b. A historical overview of the Western Province Senior Schools Sports Union. 1956 to 1973. *African Journal for Physical, Health Education, Recreation and Dance*, 15(4):701-713.

Cleophas, F.J. 2014. Opening a window on early twentieth century school sport in Cape Town society. *The International Journal of the History of Sport*, 31(15):1868–1881. https://doi.org/10.1080/09523367.2014.934679

Combeau-Mari, E. 2011. Sport and decolonisation: The community games, April 1960. *The International Journal of the History of Sport*, 28(12):1716–1726. https://doi.org/10.1080/09523367.2011.592766

Jansen, J.D. 2017. *As by fire: The end of the South African university*. Cape Town: Tafelberg.

Le Grange, L. 2016. Decolonising the university curriculum. *South African Journal of Higher Education,* 30(2):1–12.

Liss, H. 1970. *Funks & Wagnalls Encyclopedia*. p. 13.

Mignolo, W. 2007. Introduction: Coloniality of power and de-colonial thinking. *Cultural Studies,* 21(2–3):155–167. https://doi.org/10.1080/09502380601162498

Odendaal, A. 2003. *The story of an African game: Black cricketers and the unmasking of one of cricket's greatest myths, 1850–2003*. Cape Town: New Africa Books.

Odendaal, A., Reddy, K., Merret, C. & Winch, J. 2016. *Cricket and conquest: The history of South African cricket retold, volume 1, 1795–1914*. Cape Town: Human Sciences Research Council Press.

Quijano, A. 2007. Coloniality and modernity/rationality. *Cultural Studies*, 21(2–3):168–178. https://doi.org/10.1080/09502380601164353

Smith, L. 1999. *Decolonising methodologies: Research and indigenous peoples*. London: Zed Books.

Snyders, H. 2016. Old friends at the game in Africa: The origins and early development of Lacrosse in Natal, South Africa. *Sporting Traditions,* 33(2):93–109.

Wagner, J. 1993. Ignorance in educational research: Or, how can you not know that? *Educational Researcher,* 22(5):15–23. https://doi.org/10.2307/1176947

ACCOUNTS FROM THE ARENA

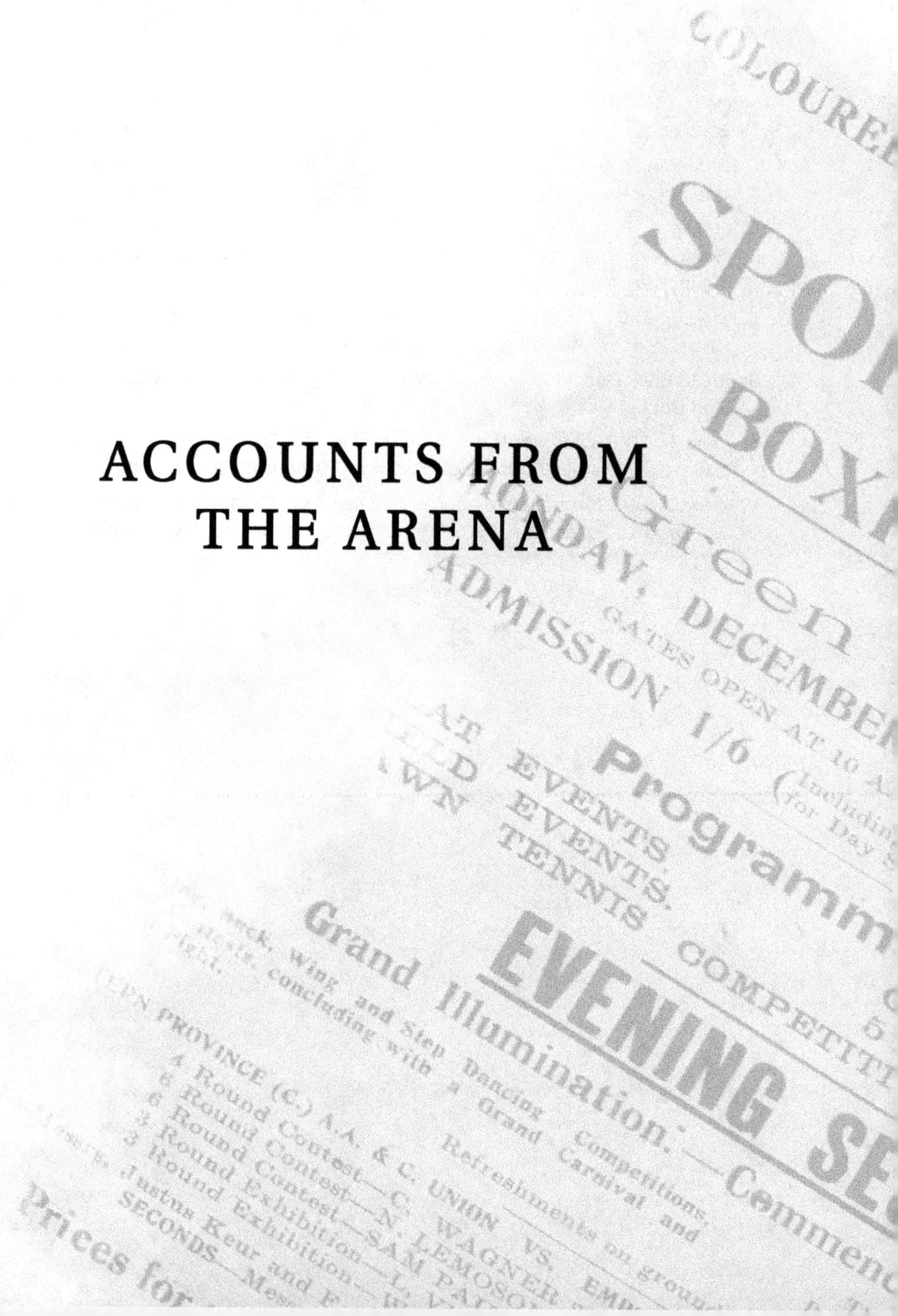

'Subservient jester'?
'Gamat' Behardien:
Reinterpreting a marginal figure in South African sport history

Hendrik Snyders

Head of Department, History, National Museum Bloemfontein and Research Associate, History Department, Stellenbosch University

Introduction

Fan studies and research into black sporting tradition and legacy is an underdeveloped field in South African sports history. This lack of activity lies at the heart of the continued existence of some sporting codes as 'unmapped landscapes' (Cleophas & Van der Merwe 2011:226). It has further aided the survival of stereotypical descriptions of black sporting personalities as 'jesters' (Odendaal 1995:29) as well as their continued existence as nicknamed shadow figures [frequently as labour auxiliaries] on the fringes of sporting history. Nauright in this regard suggested that imposed nicknames do not only camouflage identities but are indicators that 'Sixpence' the stable hand, 'Rabbit' the caddy, or 'Gamat' the 'water boy' "really belong hundreds of miles away, not in a white urban area". He further noted that racial terminology or signifiers such as 'native', 'boy' and 'non-white' (Nauright 1997:34) have a clear political function, namely to "draw whites together as a social collectivity that was different from, and as they viewed it, culturally and morally superior to, blacks". Amongst those so treated is a small group of black men who gained notoriety within the white sporting fraternity during the apartheid years but now existed as shadow figures on the fringes of South African sport history. A tendency for political correctness emerged during the 20th century of labelling such characters as 'sell-outs', 'Uncle Toms' and 'quislings'. Such descriptors invite critical ways of exploring black complicity in colonial and apartheid projects.

In their heyday, Simon ('Aasvoel') Williams, John ('Kojak') Johnson and Gasant ('Gamat') Ederoos Behardien were public personalities closely connected with their favourite [white] sports teams. Williams, the former Stellenbosch Town Crier, earned his fame as a result of being appropriated by the University of Stellenbosch rugby club during intervarsity to help to create a 'proper atmosphere' for the annual contest against archrivals Cape Town (Craven 1955:43; Smuts 1979). Johnson, in turn, is best remembered for his vocal support of the Western Province cricket team and antiques such as running onto the field of play to offer a celebratory beer to players who scored a century (*Cape Times* 2014). Behardien, in turn, is noted for executing multiple roles, ranging from official mascot to 'water boy' and baggage master for nearly fifty years within the logistics team of the Springboks, the national rugby team (Dobson 1989:171). The latter is also the most well-known character of the three individuals. Decades later, all three remain as obscure and one-dimensional as when they became footnotes in the official histories of white rugby and cricket in South Africa. This is not surprising but rather the result of the interplay between the historian's own "biographical intersections with history and social structures" and the "subject's biographies" which dictated the manner in which the subject [or non-subject] is "inserted, reinserted, or deconstructed in contexts, directions, and struggles deemed worthy of public and popular attention" (Howell 1993:200, 207). This treatment, suggested Long & Hylton (2002:89), is also typical of the situation where "symbolic boundaries let in those who resemble the hero, but exclude those who do not". The entrants in this case, however, were rendered passive and docile in line with the workings of coloniality (Bhambra 2014:116).

This chapter therefore intends to assign historical significance, in a decolonised manner, to the life and times of one individual, Gasant Ederoos Behardien, in an attempt to address marginality and obscurity in South African sport history. In the first section, I will explore Behardien's gradual conversion into 'Gamat' – a one-dimensional, subservient and exotic character ('the other'). This will be followed by a re-appraisal and re-imagination of 'Gamat' as Gasant Behardien, a man with multiple identities and agency.

'Exotic pre-match entertainer'

In 1949, the Afrikaans newspaper, *Die Burger*, described Gasant Behardien or 'Gamat', the factotum of both Western Province and the Springboks for at least three decades, as 'Player 16' – a description that predates the recent creation of Player 23 in honour of the game's fans by cellular services provider and rugby sponsor, Vodacom. This was an image carefully created over many seasons with Behardien acting the part of a mysterious yet subservient (Malay) character, equipped with mystic potions able to cast spells that could change the fortunes and influence the match outcomes of his favourite team. His appearance on match day, noted rugby historian Paul Dobson (1989:171), "was part of the delicious pre-match excitement". As such, he was regarded as an essential part of the imagery and symbols associated with both the Western Province and Springbok teams in the period leading up to the 1950s. This lay at the heart of a public outcry in 1949 during the New Zealand All Blacks tour when the Transvaal Rugby Union excluded Behardien from the Springbok setup for the second test in Johannesburg in an attempt to enforce the newly promulgated apartheid laws (*Cape Argus* 1949). The appearance of the white-coated, be-fezzed 'Gamat', noted the *Daily Advertiser* (1949), was 'a signal that the big game was about to start'. Furthermore, some of the white fans believed that his presence and 'Malay tricks' were of critical importance to a Springbok victory (Dobson 1989:171).

Research by Torgler also indicated that belief in lucky mascots are generally high amongst low-income individuals (Torgler 2007:717, 720) – exactly the category of most white rugby fans during Behardien's time. Stollznow (2010) further noted that magic and the witchdoctor are an indelible part of South African sport and that for some athletes, they are as vital as training and the involvement of the coach. During Behardien's lifetime, the practice of selling 'Azïmatz' (or charms) [pieces of paper inscribed with Arabic verses from the Holy Qur'an] for either beneficial or harmful purposes were well known. Harmful charms obtainable from 'dukums', according to Paulsen (2003:94–5), "can cause any type of harm to anybody through the medium of their satanic powers and black magic". Furthermore, it was believed that a visit to "an Azïmatz surgery can even guarantee a win at a gambling stake, or a victory in a sporting activity". The persistence of this belief and the fascination ("otherness") it held for white (mostly Christian) rugby fans, contributed to the colonisation of the historical narrative and aided its inclusion as cameos in the various centenary histories.

Coincidentally, at least two 'Gamat-like' figures found their way into early Afrikaans teenage literature with Springbok rugby as theme. Although both the fictional 'Abdol' figure and the 'gamats' or Cape Malays as a collective in the books of I.D. du Plessis, are portrayed as knowledgeable, they are also drawn as subservient and hero-worshipping fans of white rugby and its players, suggesting the absence of a similar rugby tradition amongst black folk. In I.D. du Plessis' teenage book series with its 'Springbok' rugby theme, the character 'Abdol', a subservient Malay rugby fan who idolises national rugby star 'Baas

Behardien on Rugby Duty

Willie' Venter and considered it a singular honour to carry his tog bag, bestrode the pages. Topsy Smith's rugby novel, *Tokkelossie*, published in 1946, similarly featured a subservient and overtly thankful 'Gamat-like' figure in addition to using the term "Gamat" to collectively describe Cape Town's Malay rugby supporters. Since these books were meant as educational and political instruments for the moulding of young Afrikaner men (Du Plessis 1938), it undoubtedly forms part of the colonisation project that aimed to render some opaque and knowable, and others transparent and invisible (Maldonado-Torres 2011:10).

'Subservient jester' and 'jolly hotnot?'

Judging by contemporary newspaper reports, the description of 'Gamat' as a subservient and obliging character with an overtly and sometimes excessively respectful manner and way of addressing white rugby administrators and players, is mostly accurate. A devoted fan, Behardien were on friendly terms with Bennie Osler, one of white South Africa's early rugby heroes. Behardien further had good relations with Dr Herman van Broekhuizen, former Springbok captain and Danie Craven (Springbok Coach and President of the SA Rugby Football Board). Craven, in particular, reversed Behardien's exclusion from the Springbok logistics team and raised the necessary funds from white benefactors to cover his travel costs to Port Elizabeth for the last test on 16 September 1949 against the New Zealand visitors where he led a live springbok mascot nicknamed "Gerry Geffin" onto the field (*Cape Argus* 1949). In addition, he was the only black person with access to the playing field. All others were restricted to segregated seating on a covered stand at the back of the goal posts to prevent potential racial conflict. Unperturbed by the politics around his presence, Behardien preferred to express his gratitude for the financial assistance and sidestepped the questions about the circumstances preceding his arrival. In this regard, he remarked: "I can't thank

Baas Searle and his colleagues enough for bringing me here, but silence is better than talk" (*Daily Advertiser* 1949). This response and his refusal to comment on the circumstances that led to his previous exclusion in the end proved problematic. Furthermore, the state of rugby politics also problematised Behardien's status at a time that the black rugby community attempted to establish a foothold in the international arena.

The Springbok tour to the British Isles at the end of 1951 coincided with an unsuccessful attempt by the SA Bantu Rugby Football Board (later the South African African Rugby Football Board) to send an all-black Springbok team to play either the New Zealand Maori or Fiji (Imvo 1951). As part of the initiative, an ad hoc Non-European Rugby Football Federation (NERFF) to "accentuate the spirit of unity that is the watchwords of all Non-Europeans" was established, which selected a combined non-racial African/Coloured Federation team to send overseas (Imvo 1952). This venture had to be abandoned because of government opposition, including the denial of a passport to AZ Lamani, the NERFF organiser (Wilson 2004:20). Lack of funds, political instability in the country because of the Defiance of Unjust Laws Campaign as well as opposition on the part of the white South African Rugby Football Board (SARFB) also contributed to the failure of the venture (Odendaal 1995:44, 52). Seemingly unaware or unperturbed by the anguish and frustration of his brethren, Behardien, in response to a question on the prospects of the white national team remarked, "These new Springboks, I am proud of them. And under Mr [Frank] Mellish and Baas [Danie] Craven, they are going to do well" (*Cape Argus* 1951). Behardien's comfortability with racially offensive terminology, a-political nature, reluctance to criticise apartheid and support for the all-white Springbok rugby team at a time that a growing number of black South Africans were beginning to reject the inherent racism thereof, placed Behardien diametrically opposed to those involved in the anti-apartheid struggle.

Against this background, Odendaal (1995:29) adjudged these relationships as abnormal and reflective of "the unequal and paternalistic relations that used to characterize sporting contacts between black and white at the Cape" at the time. Behardien in his view was therefore little more than a 'subservient jester' whose exclusion from the historical narrative by implication is justified. There is a suspicion that Odendaal's characterisation might have been influenced by his status as an 'engaged historian' (Guttmann 2003:363). As a [white] anti-apartheid activist, he sacrificed a potential lucrative professional cricket career under the establishment South African Cricket Union (SACU), by switching allegiance to the non-establishment SA Cricket Board of Control (SACBOC). The latter rejected all forms of segregation and its associated symbols. Thus, Odendaal rejects Behardien's exercise of 'native agency' (Clevenger 2017:14) that fostered a deliberate association with apartheid sports, turning him into a turncoat, worthy of judgment. Behardien's collective portrayals by Dobson, Parker and Odendaal, can be regarded as acts of 'stripping' and de-individualisation that have effectively turned the subject into what Gerwel (1983:33), in a different context, has called a 'jolly hotnot', and a source of mirth and rejection. It has therefore the same features as the colonising act since it also subalternised rather than humanised (Maldonado-Torres 2011:3, 9). This is also consistent with Howell's (1993:200, 207) observation with regard to the influence of the intersection between the historian's own prejudices and the production of history earlier referred to.

The above-mentioned accounts failed to take cognisance of Behardien as a person with multiple identities that extended beyond the rugby field. Contemporary evidence shows him as a successful tailor, businessperson, avid athlete and a devout Muslim. 'Gamat the Jester' therefore can serve as a lens into multiple identities and their often-neglected histories within the South African context.

Tailor and businessperson

Most reports in newspapers and rugby publications noted Behardien's status as a tailor with one unconfirmed source even referring to him as the Springboks' tailor. Contemporary photographs, in addition to showing images of Behardien in his trademark red fez and white overcoat at match day, consistently showed the subject as a well-dressed man in tailored suits. The occupation of tailor was a prominent one in the Coloured community. Together with dressmaking and baking, a lucrative profession, it offered opportunities for economic advancement beyond unskilled labour (Jeppie 1990:29). According to the historian, Mohammed Adhikari, these occupations were confined to the small elite (the emerging petty bourgeoisie) which numbered around 5% of the Coloured population during the earlier decades of the 20th century – precisely the time of Behardien's first appearance on the rugby scene. Adhikari (2002:125) further suggests that this group "assimilated Western bourgeois culture", shared its "values, aspirations and social practices" and desired "little more than to be judged on merit, to exercise citizenship rights and to win social acceptance within white middle-class society".

Behardien, judging by his presence at games all over the country, seemingly was a successful businessperson who could afford long periods away from his business while attending to his 'duties' as 'water boy', masseuse, baggage master etc. for the Springboks. In addition, he maintained a regular presence at Newlands for Western Province rugby for almost five decades. Behardien also did occasional duty in Wellington for the Boland Rugby Union (Theron 1989:59). At the time, his absence from as much as his presence at games was regarded as a newsworthy item in the local and national media. Danie Craven [Springbok Coach in 1954], with reference to Behardien's unfailing presence at matches, remarked "how he came to each place was sometimes difficult to understand" since the respective unions did not always cover the full costs of his travel and accommodation (Craven 1949:36). If one considers the costs associated with regular non-remunerative travelling and accommodation in addition to his normal domestic expenses, it is clear that Behardien had the means to finance and sustain his activities over a substantial period. A 1949 report in the *Daily Advertiser* (1949) noted that Behardien owned a shop and home, indicating that the practice of his trade was not a home-based cottage industry but one operated from separate premises as a production and retail facility (i.e. a proper factory).

Behardien – Tailor at 17 years of age
(SA Rugby Collection)

Rugby and religion

As a practising Muslim, Behardien's red fez was probably the most visible demonstration of his religious beliefs and cultural origins. The wearing of this headgear was, however, not unique since most rugby fans who were coincidentally of Muslim extraction, regularly attended matches at Newlands, Cape Town, and sported both red fezzes and 'smart gray suits'. This presence prompted Danie Craven to attempt to have the Newland's South Stand renamed the 'Malay Stand' in honour of 'those Malay supporters who he regarded as amongst the most knowledgeable people in the world" (Dobson 1989:172). The Cape Malay community in Cape Town has a strong and very distinctive rugby tradition that dates back to the 19th century. With the formation of the Western Province Coloured Rugby Football Union (established in 1885), and City & Suburban Rugby Union (established in 1898), rugby was organised along religious lines within the larger Cape Peninsula. Whereas the former catered predominantly for those of the Muslim faith, the latter restricted its membership to players of the Christian faith. "Culture, politics and even life itself was rugby," noted Nauright (1997:186) in this regard. Whether this factor had any influence on Behardien's choice of the teams that he chose to support is, however, not known.

Behardien, for the better part of his life, resided within the Strand-Somerset (formerly known as Mostert Bay) and the larger Hottentots-Holland area. This area boasted a significant Muslim (Javanese) population since the 18th century. It is also an area with its own well-established cultural institutions such as the Nurul Islam Congregation and Strand Muslim Primary School, and has a distinctive community life (Rhoda 2004). From the available evidence, rugby in the area was established at an early stage, and by 1937, the region boasted its own coordinating structure, the Somerset West & Districts Rugby Football Union. Behardien is also on record as saying that he preferred his sons to play rugby instead of soccer. An attempt by one of his children to make a different choice resulted in active and seemingly aggressive parental disapproval and discouragement (*Daily Advertiser* 1949). Nauright (1997:188) remarked in this regard that "toughness and physicality in sporting practice suggested that muscular prowess was central in male identity formation and cultural expression in the Muslim-dominated working-class areas of Cape Town".

Athletics, courteous conduct and personal prowess

Black communities in the Cape Colony and later the Cape Province took an early interest in English sports such as football (soccer), rugby, cricket and athletics [track and field]. Whereas rugby was formally organised on a proto-national basis with the founding of the South African Coloured Rugby Football Board (SACRFB) in 1896, a year earlier, the Cape Colony Amateur Athletic and Cycling Union was established. By 1898 another body, the Good Hope Athletic and Cycling Club (Coloured) was established 'to provide participation opportunities for Cape Coloureds' and by the 1920s when Behardien entered formal athletics as a competitive walker, the sport was thoroughly segregated. At this stage it is not certain whether he belonged to any of the established athletic clubs that competed on Bank, Weiner, Boxing Day and other events hosted in Cape Town and the surrounding areas. On the symbolic level, walking, noted Solnit (2000:29), represented an "engagement of the body and the mind with the world, of knowing the world through the body and the body through the world".

The various organisations responsible for the primary organisation of Coloured sport in the Cape Colony, almost without exception, emphasised good conduct and discipline, race pride, prowess and compliance with all rules and regulations. Athletics itself, according to the African Political Organisation (APO), the chief campaigner for racial equality from the start of the 20th century, was a "clean, honest and manly sport" (APO 1913:11) and therefore worth pursuing. Solnit (2000:29) in turn suggested that walking as a recreational and sporting activity provided individuals with an instrument to express their presence and awareness of the world.

Behardien's chosen discipline, walking, was a popular item amongst athletes and following the successes achieved by Cecil Charles McMaster, the white South African champion walker in the 3000m and 10 kilometre distances at the Olympic Games in Antwerpen (1920) and Paris (1924), the discipline started to attract new attention and increased participation. Although the establishment of an organisation that promoted Olympism within the black sports fraternity was only established years later, most South Africans were aware of the prestige associated with participation in the Olympic Games event ever since 'South Africa' made its first official appearance at the Games in 1908. Contemporary newspapers also carried regular reports about athletes and events in general and, as a matter of routine, regularly compared white and black achievement. Newspapers even thought it important to offer coaching advice to active athletes and promoted the notion of scientific training to raise the standards of participation (Cleophas 2010:624–5). The inauguration of a McMaster Trophy for competitive walking amongst non-white athletes therefore came as no surprise. According to notes by Dr Danie Craven in the Springbok Rugby Museum Archive Collection, Behardien won this trophy regularly between the 1920s and 1930s to establish his own claim to fame. Walking is an item in the Olympic Games programme that required:

> no visible (to the human eye) loss of contact with the ground should occur and that the leg must be straightened from first contact with the ground until the vertical upright position… [and] it is crucial that the athlete can maintain a fast but submaximal speed that wastes as little energy as possible" (Hanley & Bissas 2016:2).

Gasant Behardien – Competitive walker accompanied by assistants and technical judges (SA Rugby Collection)

Successful participation therefore required strict adherence to technical requirements, and an advanced level of technical prowess and mastery. These requirements mirrored those required of tradesmen in an era of high quality as well as those expected of white sportsmen during an era in which sporting prowess served as entry requirement for full citizenship. Behardien's choice of a sport with very high technical requirements is consistent with his choice of trade as a tailor where accuracy is a non-negotiable. Similarly, the endurance aspect of the sport mirrored that of rugby that was for a long time regarded as the ultimate manly sport. Given the total lack of official archives from the athletics bodies in question, it is, however, not possible to fully reconstruct the detail of Behardien's track and field career.

Conclusion

Sport fans are an integral part of a country's sport history and their story and life experiences are of as much importance as those of the super stars. Their life stories could and should equally serve as a lens through which to look into different aspects of society. They can also make a significant contribution to "directly challenging historical practices, beliefs, and ideas that underpin the production of sport history" (Phillips 2001:327). As a result, their re-imagining and humanisation is of the utmost importance. The case of Gasant 'Gamat' Cderoos Behardien reveals both the negative and marginalising consequences of racial and other forms of stereotyping. It further indicates how the deliberate omission of substantive facts about real persons, together with the under-emphasis of their individual and personal inter-relationships, stripped the affected from their agency and relegated them to the fringes of history. Admittedly, all actions have consequences which, in Behardien's case, is amply demonstrated by his deliberate avoidance of all things political and his accommodating of the 'unpopular.' However, going against the stream/grain is not a sufficient excuse to marginalise, stereotype or vilify individuals for their position at critical times during the course of history.

Behardien was a product of his time and part of a generation who have worked ceaselessly to demonstrate not only their manliness but also their fitness for inclusion as equal citizens into white society. This is amply demonstrated through his choice of sport and his affinity for activities that required technical mastery. Winning competitions such as the McMaster Trophy strengthened this claim and brought further recognition from those such as Craven who were internationally respected administrators. His courteous manner and close adherence to the social conventions of the time as well as his submissiveness, when required, and overt display of gratitude, were no different from that displayed by his non-political peers. Behardien was rooted in his community and succeeded in achieving a measure of economic prosperity that allowed him financial independence and the ability to pursue his passion for rugby for more than three decades. This stands in stark contrast to the stereotyped portrayal of the individual which re-emphasised historian Mewett's contention that the "social positioning of those doing the remembering influences the interpretations that they place on the past and the uses to which they are put in the present" (Mewett 2000: 1).

References

Abel, E.L. & Kruger, M.L. 2006. Nicknames increase longevity. *OMEGA-Journal of Death and Dying*, 53(3):243-248. https://doi.org/10.2190/7NTC-0K26-V9RL-57PN

Adhikari, M. 2002. Hope, fear, shame, frustration: Continuity and change in the expression of Coloured identity in white supremacist South Africa, 1910–1994. Unpublished PhD dissertation (Historical Studies), University of Cape Town, July.

"All roads lead to Port Elizabeth", *Imvo Zabantsundu*, 2 June 1951.

A.P.O. Official Organ of the African People's Organisation, 6 September 1913.

Bhambra, G.K. 2014. Postcolonial and Decolonial dialogues. *Postcolonial Studies*, 17(2):115-121. https://doi.org/10.1080/13688790.2014.966414

Bizcommunity, 2009. "Vodacom continues the Player 23 story", 8 June. Available from http://www.bizcommunity.com. [Accessed 15 August 2017].

Booley, M. 1998. *Forgotten Heroes: History of Black Rugby* 1882–1992, Cape Town: M. Booley Publications.

Booyens, B. 1975. *Danie Craven*. Cape Town: Suid-Afrikaanse Rugbyraad.

Cleophas, F.J. & Van der Merwe, F.J.G. 2009. A historical overview of the Western Province Senior Schools Sports Union, 1956 to 1973. *African Journal for Physical, Health Education, Recreation and Dance (AJPHERD)*, 15(4) (December):701-713.

Cleophas, F.J. & Van der Merwe, F.J.G. 2010. The African Political Organisation's contribution to South African sport, 1914–1915: Part III. *African Journal for Physical, Health Education, Recreation and Dance (AJPHERD)*, 16(4) (December):622-641.

Cleophas, F.J. 2016. Exploring African-American Influences on Athletics in the Cape Colony, South Africa. *The International Journal of the History of Sport*, 33(15): 1700-1716. https://doi.org/10.1080/09523367.2017.1294582

Cleophas, F.J. & Van der Merwe, F.J.G. 2011. Mapping out an obscured South African sport history landscape through Edward Henderson. *African Journal for Physical, Health Education, Recreation and Dance (AJPHERD)*, 17(2) (June):226-238.

Clevenger, S.M. 2017. Sport history, modernity and the logic of coloniality: a case for decoloniality. *Rethinking History: The Journal of Theory and Practice*, 21(4):586–605. https://doi.org/10.1080/13642529.2017.1326696

Craven, D.H. 1955. *Met die Maties op die Rugby Veld 1880–1955*, Kaapstad: Nasionale Boekhandel.

Craven, D.H. 1954. *Springbok Story 1949–1954*. Cape Town: R. Beerman Publishers.

De Wet, W. 2016. Tendense in populêre werke oor Suid-Afrikaanse rugby, 1948–1995: 'n Historiografiese Studie. *Historia* 61(1):113–131. https://doi.org/10.17159/2309-8392/2016/v61n1a9

Dobson, P. (ed.). 1989. *Rugby in South Africa: A History, 1861–1988*. Cape Town: SA Rugby Board.

Dobson, P. 1994. Doc: *The life of Danie Craven*. Cape Town: Human & Rousseau.

Du Plessis, I.D. 1938. *Die Silwervaring – 'n rugby verhaal*. Kaapstad, Bloemfontein & Port Elizabeth.

Du Plessis, I.D. 1941. *Rugby in Rio*. Kaapstad: Nasionale Pers.

Du Plessis, I.D. 1980? *Die Rugby Kroon*. Kaapstad: Malherbe.

Du Plessis, I.D. 1934. *Springbok: 'n Rugby Verhaal*. Kaapstad: Nasionale Pers.

"East London venue for Fifth Test trials", *Imvo Zabantsundu*, 2 August 1952.

Fletcher, M.W. 2012. *"These whites never come to our game. What do they know about our soccer?": Soccer Fandom, Race, and the Rainbow Nation in South Africa*. PhD diss., University of Edinburgh.

"Fourth Test win by S. Africa", *Cape Argus*, 17 September 1949.

"Gamat will herald the start of tomorrow's big game." *Daily Advertiser*, 16 September 1949.

"Gamat's heart will be in England with the team." *Cape Argus*, 1951.

Greyvenstein, C. 1970. *The Bennie Osler Story*. Cape Town: Howard Timmins.

Gammon, S.J. 2014. Heroes as heritage: The commoditization of sporting achievement. *Journal of Heritage Tourism*, 9(3):246–256. https://doi.org/10.1080/1743873X.2014.904321

Gerwel, G.J. 1983. *Literatuur en apartheid*. Bellville. Kampen-Uitgewers.

Guttmann, A. 2003. Sport, politics and the engaged historian. *Journal of Contemporary History* 38(3):363–375. https://doi.org/10.1177/0022009403038003002

Hanley, B. & Bissas, A. 2016. Ground reaction forces of Olympic and World Championship race walkers. *European Journal of Sport Science*, 16(1). Available from http://eprints.leedsbeckett.ac.uk/128/1/Ground%20reaction%20forces%20of%20Olympic%20and%20World%20Championship%20race%20walkers.pdf. (Accessed 02 January 2018). https://doi.org/10.1080/17461391.2014.984769

Hassan, D. 2013. Introduction: What makes a sporting icon? *Sport in History*, 33(4):417–426. https://doi.org/10.1057/9781137350091.0005

Howell, J.W. 1993. Evaluating sport hero/ines: Contents, forms, and social relations. *Kinesiology*, Paper 11. http://repository.usfca.edu/ess/11

Hussey, H.H. 1974. Sports and Streaking. *JAMA* 228(4):499–500. https://doi.org/10.1001/jama.228.4.499

Jeppie, S. 1990. *The class, colour and gender of carnival: aspects of a cultural form in inner Cape Town, c.1939 – c.1959*. Paper presented on Occasion of the 'Structure and Experience in the Making of Apartheid' Conference: 6–10 February 1990, History Workshop: University of the Witwatersrand.

Lewis, J.M. 2007. *Sports fan violence in North America*. Rowman & Littlefield Publishers.

Long, J. & Hylton, K. 2002. Shades of white: An examination of whiteness in Sport. *Leisure Studies*, 21:87–103. https://doi.org/10.1080/02614360210152575

MacLean, M. 1996. Of Fans and a Bright Future. *Sporting Traditions*, 13(1) (November):139–144.

Maldonado-Torres, N. 2011. Thinking through the Decolonial Turn: Post-continental interventions in theory, philosophy, and critique – An introduction. *Transmodernity*, (Fall):1–15.

Mewett, P.G. 2000. History in the Making and the Making of History: Stories and the social construction of a sport. *Sporting Traditions*, 17(1) (November):1–18.

Nauright, J. 1997. *Sport, Cultures and Identities in South Africa*. Cape Town & Johannesburg: David Phillip.

Nauright, J. 1997. Masculinity, Muscular Islam and Popular Culture: 'Coloured' Rugby's Cultural Symbolism in Working-class Cape Town c. 1930-70. *The International Journal of the History of Sport*, 14(1) (April):184-190. https://doi.org/10.1080/09523369708713972

Odendaal, A. 1995. 'The thing that is not round': The untold story of black rugby in South Africa, in A.M. Grundlingh, A.A. Odendaal & B. Spies, *Beyond the Tryline: Rugby and South African Society*. Johannesburg: Ravan Press.

"One springbok did not even see the test", *Cape Argus*, 17 September 1949.

Parker, A.C. 1983. *Western Province Rugby Centenary 1883-1983*. Cape Town: WPRFU.

Partridge, T. 1991. *A life in rugby*. Cape Town: Southern Book Publishers.

Paulsen, M.A. 2003. *The Malay community of Gauteng: Syncretism, beliefs, customs and development*. PhD dissertation. University of Johannesburg.

Phillips, M.G. 2001. Deconstructing Sport History: The Postmodern Challenge. *Journal of Sport History*, 28(3) (Fall):327-343.

'Player 16.' *Die Burger*. 18 July 1949.

Real, M.R. & Mechikoff, R.A. 1992. Deep fan: Mythic identification, technology, and advertising in spectator sports, *Sociology of Sport Journal*, (9)4:323-339.

Rhoda, E. *The Origin of the Rhoda Family of the Strand*. Available from https://family. morkel.net/wp-content/uploads/Rhoda-Family-Origins-.pdf. Accessed 15 August 2017. 10.1123/ssj.9.4.323

Rugby365, 2013. Rugby historian Paul Dobson reflects on the opening of the Bok Experience museum. Available from http://www.rugby365.com/article/56394-bok-heritage-alive. Accessed 15 August 2017.

SA Rugby Union (SARU), Springbok Experience Museum Photographic Collection.

Smith, I. "Eddie may give Smithy a heads-up." *Cape Times*, 12 February 2013 and "'Kojak' would be smiling." *Cape Argus*, 15 December 2014. Available from http://www.elitecc. co.za/news/20021118.html. Accessed 15 August 2017.

Smuts, F. 1979. *Stellenbosch Drie Eeue*. Stellenbosch: Stadsraad.

Snyders, H. 2015. Rugby, national pride and the struggle of Black South Africans for international recognition, 1897-1992, *Sporting Traditions* 32(1):95-122.

Smith, T. 1946. *Ons Springbok-rugbyspelers en Tokkelossie*. Johannesburg: Afrikaanse Pers-Boekhandel.

Smith, T. 1947. *Draers van die Groen en Goud*. Johannesburg: Afrikaanse Pers Boekhandel.

Solnit, R. 2000. *Wanderlust: A History of Walking*. New York: Penguin.

Springbok Experience Museum Collection. Available from Museum at the V &A Waterfront, Cape Town.

Stollznow, K. 2010. "Football Gazing: Sport and superstitions in South Africa." *Skeptical Enquirer*, June 22. Available: https://www.csicop.org/specialarticles/show/football_gazing_sports_and_superstitions_in_south_africa. [Accessed 1 March 2018].

Strong, P.T. 2004. The mascot slot: Cultural citizenship, political correctness, and pseudo-Indian sports symbols. *Journal of Sport and Social Issues*, 28(1):79-87. 10.1177/0193732503261672

Theron, P. 1989. *Boland Rugby: Die Eerste Halfeeu*. Wellington: Boland RFU.

Torglo, B. 2007. Determinants of superstition. *The Journal of Socio-Economics 36*:713–733. 10.1016/j.socec.2007.01.007

Toriola, A.L. & Nongogo, P. 2014. Xhosa people and the rugby game: diffusion of sport in the Eastern Cape of South Africa under colonial and apartheid eras. *African Journal for Physical Health Education, Recreation and Dance*, 20(3):1293–1319.

Vaczi, M. 2016. Dangerous liaisons, fatal women: The fear and fantasy of soccer wives and girlfriends in Spain. *International Review for the Sociology of Sport*, 51(3):299–313. 10.1177/1012690214524756

Wilson, H. 2004. South African Rugby Union/SARU. Unpublished manuscript.

Black Athletics in Cape Town prior to 1920

Francois Cleophas
Senior lecturer, Sport History, Department of Sport Science, Stellenbosch University

Introduction

This chapter presents a historical-social account of athletics in the Cape Colony and Province until 1920 and extends on a growing academic interest in a history of athletics in Cape Town's traditionally marginalised communities. It extends on the existing formal corpus of works on South African colonial athletic history (Cleophas & Van der Merwe 2010a; Cleophas & Van der Merwe 2010b; Cleophas 2011; Cleophas 2013a; Cleophas 2013b; Cleophas 2013b; Coghlan 1986; Van der Merwe & Venter 1987; Van der Merwe 1987). It also attempts to present an athletic history that opens windows on colonial society. Further, it also places black athletics at the centre of analysis. As such, it counters works that degenerate 19th and early 20th century black athletics completely or analyse the subject as an addendum to white history (see Steyn 2015:18–19; Vogt 1951:37-39).

A decolonised athletic narrative is one that advances the historical accounts of marginalised groups. These accounts are not forced narratives or artificial impositions of people but a seamless tapestry of events (Odendaal 2017). Previous narratives advanced Eurocentric interests that marginalised blacks and women (see Parker 1897; Springboks past and present, 1947). According to the cricket historian, André Odendaal, white South Africans were complacent about this situation and because of that they made other people invisible (Odendaal 2017).

Dutch colonial period (1652–1795; 1803–1806)

No evidence has yet been found that formal athletic events were held during the Dutch colonial period (1652–1795; 1803–1805). The novelist, Dan Sleigh, wrote that during the governorship period of Louis van Assenburgh, (1 February 1708 – 27 December 1711) there was an annual tournament that included horse races. By 1738 bull fights featured as entertainment and a fictitious long-distance runner, Jan Ras, featured in his novel (Sleigh 1973: inside cover, 6). Tournaments were the equivalent of modern-day sports events (Van der Merwe 2007:80).

British colonial period (1806 onwards)

Horseracing was popular on isolated border settlements. Once or twice a year, in line with British custom, a week-long series of races were held that were accompanied by fairs that allowed for much dancing and drinking. Coloured servant jockeys were used to show off the prowess of the owner and a fat-smeared piglet was let loose for the local Khoi who could take it home if it was caught by him or her. Often, as was the case in Somerset-East in 1826, the strict Scottish Presbyterian ministers denied church members the partaking of the sacrament if they participated in these fairs (Muller 1974:166).

During the 19th century most athletic meetings in Cape Town and surrounds were similar to the rural sports in England which were connected to festivals (Van der Merwe 2007:156). Thus, in 1897, the Paarl District Cricket Club planned its 'Annual Athletic Sports' for the afternoon of its Agricultural Show on 21 January under the auspicies of the Cape Colony Amateur Athletics and Cycling Association. The programme of this cricket club also included foot, hurdle and cycle races (*Cape Times* 1897:4). Athletics also had a broad reference. Thus, when Tom Burrows set up a world record in Indian club swinging in May 1897 at the Alhambra Music Hall in Cape Town, he was reported on as a 'far-famed British expert on a very fascinating branch of athletics' (Burrows n.d.:11). According to the sport historians, Van der Merwe and Venter, non-whites competed against whites, although this was the exception to the rule at these festivals (Van der Merwe & Venter 1987:78). At a rural sport event held to celebrate the marriage of the Prince of Wales in 1863, on the Grand Parade in Cape Town, Simeon, a Coloured, competed and gained first place in the hurdles event. The sports day had all the elements of an Englishman's holiday: greasy pole, a pig with a greasy tail, sword dancing and jumping in sacks. Afterwards, a dinner was held at the Paddock at which 350 persons sat down and the Governor took the chair (*Cape Argus* 1863:1).

In the nineteenth century Anglo-Saxon world, cricket was a very important game at black colleges, such as Zonnebloem (Odendaal 2003:25). However, athletics was part of the cultural experience at Zonnebloem and past students engaged in running, throwing and jumping at St. Mark's Mission station in the Eastern Cape between 3 and 5 November 1869 (Hodgson, 1975:538). The Cape Colony had a marked English liberal sport tradition with a custom of holding a special event for Coloureds at athletic meetings (*Cradock Register* 1873:3). In some cases whites objected and in 1873 some of them boycotted a sports meeting to celebrate the Queen's birthday in Clanwilliam because Coloureds were permitted to compete (*Cape Argus* 1873:1, 4). During the 19th century, organised sport was a rarity amongst colonists who were living under rural conditions and was usually only practised on festive occasions (Du Toit 1942). Such informal activity did not need clubs, but once a formal level of organisation was required, then clubs developed. Clubs enabled people with a common purpose to come together (Vamplew 2013). To date, the oldest known athletic club in Cape Town was the Cape Town Athletic Club that held its first meeting on 27 November 1875 (*Cape Argus* 1875:1).

The athletic historian, Doug Coghlan, reckons the track meeting organised by the Good Hope Athletic (Coloured) Club (GHACC) on 24 October 1898 was the start of organised athletics in Cape Town's Coloured community (Coghlan 1986:450). Although the GHACC meeting was advertised as a Malay (Muslim) event, accommodation was also made for non-Malays. One the two cyclists, A.J. Moko and Z. Zitayi, came from the African community (*Cape Times* 1898:6). The organisation of the meeting was however largely in the hands of white middle-class officials and *The Cape Times* reported on it more as a festive occasion than an athletic meeting:

> *Abdol* and *Hadjie* were *en fete* when the Malay community held an athletic and cycling meeting at the Green Point Track ... the spectators were dressed in all glory of beautiful costume which *Hadjie* delights in ... with the sober *fez* of their lords ... and a party of wandering musicians lent a more or less dolorous programme of instrumental music (*Cape Times* 1898:6).

An indication of the festive spirit was further highlighted by the holding of a potato race, a tug-of-war between the Good Hope and Arabian Football Clubs, and a half-mile walk in Malay shoes (*kaparings*) (*Cape Times* 1898:6). The GHACC held another meeting on 22 April 1899 at the Green Point Track. Scant information about this meeting exists in the media where W. Light, the groundsman, challenged the Malay champion to a quarter-mile race and several gentlemen of the leading cycling clubs consented to conduct the meeting (*Cape Argus* 1899:5 & *Cape Times* 1899:4). This club held one more meeting after which the second South African War (1899–1902) interrupted it's activities. Organised athletics in the Coloured community emerged in a time period, the last decade of the 19th century, when national political organisation was taking root (Lewis 1987:10).

1901 onwards

In May 1901, John Tobin, a local Coloured businessman, started convening his Stone meetings where he stressed black self-help and upliftment (Lewis 1987:18). This was the same year that the Western Province Amateur Athletic & Cycling Union (Coloured) (WPAA&CA) (C) was established. There were however clubs and athletes that competed outside the WPAA&CA (C). The Paarl Club initially did not affiliate to the Association and therefore the Association barred athletes from participating in meetings organised by the Paarl Club. These athletes were reinstated in 1920 (*SA Clarion* 1920b:15). There were two Paarl athletic clubs by 1920, one whose athletes competed in the competitions of the WPAA&CA (C) and another that, in all likelihood, applied segregation and was established in 1896 (Vogt 1950:37).

Tobin was also the track referee at the inaugural athletic meeting of the (WPAA&CA) (C) on 7 July 1902. This meeting was possibly part of the King Edward VII Coronation celebrations that were organised at the Green Point Track (Cleophas & Van der Merwe 2012:49). He was also involved in the embroyonic socialist activity in Cape Town. Tobin helped established the African Political Organisation (later African People's Organisation) (A.P.O) in 1902 which later held meetings in the Socialist Hall in Buitenkant Street, Cape Town (A.P.O 1909a:2). Many of the other officials at the 1902 track meeting were also involved in community activities. Morris Alexander was the patron at the inception of the WPAA&CA (C) (*SA Clarion* 1919g:16). Alexander was a white liberal parliamentarian who, as Van der Ross (1986:41) observes, "fought for the rights of non-whites but in vain". He identified himself with sport projects within the Coloured community. It has been documented that he supported the former non-white Zonnebloem College track sprinter, Harold Cressy, in his struggle to be admitted to the South African College School (SACS) (Adhikari 2002:89; Adhikari 2000:11). Besides his involvement with the WPAA&CA he also attached his name to a school athletic competition organised by the Teachers' League of South Africa (TLSA) (Cleophas 2014:1870), as well as the Western Province Football Association (Coloured) (Cleophas 2010a:165). With increasing segregation at the turn of the 20th century, ambitious Coloured men found they were being excluded from holding public positions. They turned to sport and a well-known soccer administrator, Stephan Reagon, stated: '… if you cannot be the premier of South Africa, you can certainly be determined to become the president of the Western Province Coloured Football Association (Cleophas 2015:454). The full complement of officials at the 7 July 1902 athletics meeting were: John Tobin (referee); M. Franciscus, J. Bruyns (senior), C. Jacobs and W.J. Williams (judges), J. Bruyns and Matthew Fredericks (treasurer and handicapper); M.J. Wilson (starter); W. Bonzaaier (timekeeper); Simon Geyer (lap scorer); Peter Smeda (clerk of the course); P. Ryan, Carel Carelse and H. Isaacs (corner judges); J. Poggenpoel and J. Mackman (competitor stewards) and J. Bruyns (secretary). Some of these officials were prominent public personalities at the time:

C. Jacobs

This possibly was Christian George Jacobs, who was part of a three-man delegation, alongside Francis Peregrino and William Collins, to the Duke and Duchess of Cornwall and York during a royal visit to Cape Town in August 1901 (*South African Spectator* 1901:5). Jacobs was also secretary of the YMCA (Coloured) (*South African Spectator* 25 January 1902:3).

Matthew J. Fredericks

Matthew Jacobus Fredericks, an insurance agent by profession, was born in Cape Town in 1872 and died in Wetton on 14 June 1936 (Western Cape Archives and Records Services, MOOC 6/9/4782). He was a key figure in the APO and served as general secretary of the APO from 1903 until his death in 1936 (Adhikari 2005:123).

M.J. Wilson

This possibly was Jonathan Wilson, who was part of a Cape Town Welcoming Reception Committee in Cape Town for the 1909 African Political Organisation (APO) delegation returning from London (A.P.O. 1909b:6). Wilson was "a resident in Green Point, for years a contractor at the docks and one of the best known Coloured men in Cape Town and it was said that he was one the largest employers of labour" (*South African Spectator* 1902:6).

Simon Geyer

Simon Frederick Geyer, also known as Daddy Jim, was president and treasurer of the WPAA&CA from 1903 onwards (*SA Clarion* 1920e:15), a position he was still holding in 1920 (*SA Clarion*, 1920f:15). He was also a member of the Western Province Tennis Club (*SA Clarion*, 1920a:15). In 1919 he was the organiser of a successful boxing tournament, when such events were relatively scarce in the Coloured community (Cleophas 2011:711–712). His death notice states he was born in Uitenhage in 1871 and passed away on 24 December 1943 in Sussex Street, Claremont. He was also associated with the St David's Lodge Ancient Order of Africa Free Gardeners and the Cape Friendlies Society (Western Cape Archives and Records Services, MOOC 6/9/10596).

Peter Smeda

Peter Smeda became an APO executive member in 1906 and was the secretary of the Cape Town branch in 1909 (Adhikari 1996:52; Van der Ross, 1975:19).

P.C. Ryan

P.C. Ryan served on the first executive of the Cape Corps and Gifts Committee in 1915 (Difford 1920:322). He was also an officer in the Church Lads' Brigade (*SA Clarion* 1920a:2).

J. Poggenpoel

Jacobus Andrew Poggenpoel, a wagon builder and blacksmith by profession, was born in Cape Town in 1869 and died in Grassy Park on 25 March 1936 (Western Cape Archives and Records Services, MOOC 6/9/ 4776). He was an APO stalwart who resigned from the organisation in 1910 and then supported the National Party (Adhikari 1996:121). This support took the form of a Coloured wing of the National Party, the United Afrikaner League (UAL) that supported segregation (Adhikari 2002:89). He held a leading position in the Coloured Insurance Company (Van der Ross 1986:80).

After the South African War, segregation in sport was established more firmly. When the Orange River Colony A.A. and C.A. requested information from the South African Amateur Athletic and Cycling Association (SAAA&CA) in 1904 about the participation of 'natives' in athletic meetings, the Orange River Colony was discouraged from holding 'mixed' athletic meetings. This attitude would not have been different in the Cape Colony since it was also represented on the SAAA&CA (Le Roux 1984:11). The *SA Clarion* listed the following athletes as outstanding during this period: J.F. Bruyns, Moos Franciscus, Simon Geyer, Simon Knoll, Joe Rive, Peter Smeda and Jack (John) Tobin (*SA Clarion* 1920d:8). Despite segregation measures that counted against them, these athletes nearly always appeared with symbols of 'public respectability'.

This track meeting took place four months before the APO was established on 30 September 1902 with Collins as president and Tobin as vice-president (Lewis 1987:20). Although there was a visible presence of politicians in the WPAA&CA (C), sport participation in the Western Cape, as elsewhere in the world, was promoted largely by motives of morals and culture, not

Founder members of the WPAACA(C) in public appearance of respectability
(SA Clarion, 1919g:12)

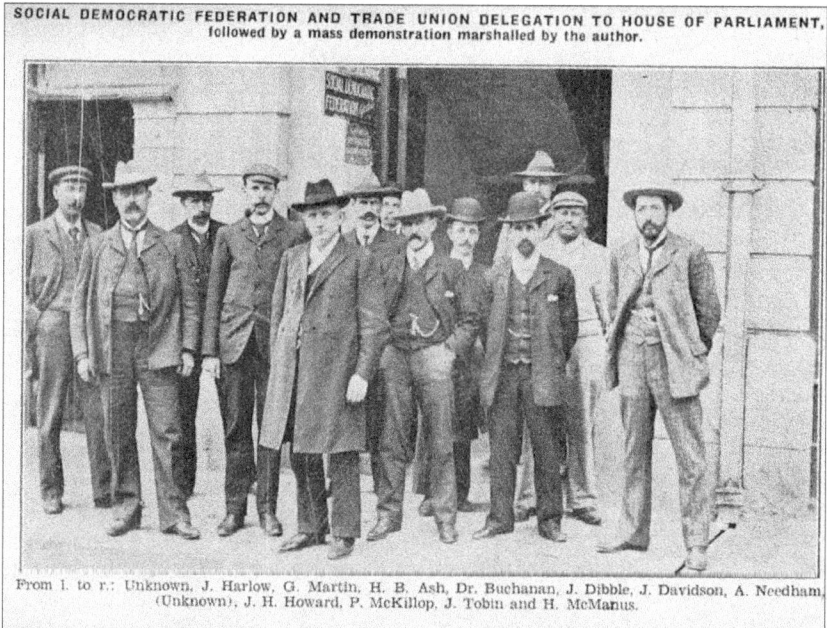

John Tobin, second from right, with a Socialist Democratic Federation delegation
(Harrison, 194?:7)

The Coronation Physical Training competition (*Cape Argus Weekly*, 2 July 1902:19). Displays
of colonial loyalty at the same venue one week before the inaugural WPAA&CA (C) meeting

Inaugural WPAA&CA (C) athletic meeting
(*Cape Argus Weekly*, 9 July 1902:34)

politics (Du Toit 1942:i). The APO was controlled by the elite within the Coloured community and so was the WPAA&CA (C). Prior to the Second World War, the APO controlled the organised cultural affairs of the Coloured people, including athletics. When problems arose with clubs operating outside the WPAA&CA (C), athletes turned to the APO.

The Paarl Club initially did not affiliate to the Association and therefore the Association penalised athletes from participating in meetings organised by this club (*SA Clarion* 1920b:15). In 1910, an annual Paarl Sports Day for Coloured athletes was held for the first time under the auspices of the association (*Cape Standard* 1945:9). A track sprinter with the surname Flotman, who was part of the Cape Corps Battalion serving in France during the First World War and a member of the Spes Bona Athletic and Cycling Club (*SA Clarion* 1920e:14; Cleophas 2010:162), appealed to the APO to arrange an athletic competition after he was debarred from the Paarl Sports New Year's Day meeting in 1910. He also claimed that the Sea Point athletes made a reputation for themselves for running (APO 1910: 15). These athletes were reinstated in 1920 (*SA Clarion* 1920b:15).

The Great War (1914–1918)

During the war, activities came to a virtual standstill. Although the Association retained the term 'cycling', the cyclists broke away from the union, taking with it desperately needed income. The Spanish influenza and a poor bank balance were some of the other adversities faced by the union (*SA Clarion* 1920d:8). In 1915 an athletic meeting, under the auspices of the Association, was held in support of the Govenor-General's Fund. This meeting was run at a financial loss (*SA Clarion* 1919g:16). A major track and field event, according to the *SA Clarion*, took place in Cape Town in 1916 but there was a lapse of four years before another was organised (*SA Clarion* 1920c:15). The year, 1917, was devoted to the assistance of the Cape Corps Gifts and Comforts Fund while, owing to the Spanish influenza of 1918, no athletic meeting was held. A planned Boxing Day meeting was cancelled in favour of fund-raising efforts for the Governor-General's Fund (*SA Clarion* 1919g:16).

The first WPAA&CA (Coloured) AGM, after the war, was held on Monday 30 June 1919 at 58b Loop Street, Cape Town (*SA Clarion* 1919c:14). This was the address of the offices of the APO. Monthly committee meetings were held at the home of the president, Simon Geyer (*SA Clarion* 1919d:10). The WPAA&CA(C) made use of the Cape Province Amateur Athletics and Cycling Union rules at a time when the secretary was A.D. Wentzel (*SA Clarion* 1919e:13). A series of road races were organised in Cape Town by the Salford Harriers that year. On 4 and 29 April 1919, this club staged a 3-mile inter-club handicap road race and 880 yards handicap road race. The results were: 3km road race (1st H. Herman in 16 min.3/5 sec., 2nd G. Canterbury and 3rd F. Bakers); 880 yards (1st Kingsley in 2 min. 23 3/5sec., 2nd E. Davids and 3rd G. Canteberry) (*SA Clarion* 1919b:16). These events retained much of the pre-war Games Culture but started moving towards becoming fully fledged athletic meetings as we know them today. It was also true that by 1920, cycling was the dominant code above athletics and the majority of the WPAA&CA (C) were cyclists rather than athletes. That year the executive consisted of: S.F. Geyer (president and treasurer); C.M. Dantu (also vice-president of the City Cricket League) (*SA Clarion* 1919f:2); Matt Fredericks; William Goliath; Stephen Reagon (in 1934 he was the vice president of the Cape Peninsula Lawn Tennis Union) (*Sun* 1934:2) and C. Shuter (vice-presidents); A.S. Williams of the Y.M.C.A. (chairman in the place of H. Connolly), W.H. Muller of Salfords (vice chairman), R. Beyers, J.F. Bruyns, J. Crane, W. van Kesteren, Justus Keur, B. Pierce, Ben Keis/Kies (all cyclists) and A.D. Wentzel (secretary) (*SA Clarion* 1920d:8).

WPAA&CA (C) meeting in 1920 displaying games culture
(*SA Clarion*, 1920f:3)

Conclusion

This reconstructed narrative attempted to create a historical account of black athletics in Cape Town prior to 1920 by recalling events and individuals who were, until now, left outside mainstream sport history. Their stories are not artificial and mitigate against arguments of black absence in South African athletic history. It was shown how the early athletic officials operated with cultural and moral agency. Although they also held political office, they tended to avoid mixing politics and athletics. The early organisation of athletics in Cape Town's Coloured community thus internalised and promoted British values. What is evident, though, is that the omission of white officials at the first official WPAA&CA (C) track meeting was an attempt to show black political independence by means of self-reliance. Through this historical analysis of the WPAA&CA (C), a window on colonial society is opened for historians dedicated on perusing further decolonisation themes in sport.

References

Adhikari, M. 1996. Straatpraatjies. In M. Adhikari (ed.). *Straatpraatjies: Language, Politics and Popular Culture in Cape Town, 1909–1922*. Cape Town: J.L. van Schaik Publishers:19–128.

Adhikari, M. 2000. *Against the current. A biography of Harold Cressy, 1889–1916*. Cape Town: Juta Publishers.

Adhikari, M. 2002. *Dr. Abdurahman. A biographical memoir by JH Raynard*. Cape Town: Friends of the National Library of South Africa.

Adhikari, M. 2005. *Not White enough, not Black enough. Racial identity in the South African Coloured Community*. Cape Town: Double Storey Books.

A.P.O. Official Organ of the African Political Organisation. 1909a. 24 May.

A.P.O. Official Organ of the African Political Organisation. 1909b. 25 September.

A.P.O. Official Organ of the African Political Organisation. 1910. 15 January.

Booth, D. 2005. *The field. Truth and fiction in sport history*. London: Routledge.

Burrows, T. n.d. *The text-book of club-swinging*. London: Athletic.

Cape Argus, The. Marriage Festival Supplement. 1863. 21 May.

Cape Argus, The. 1873. 1 July.

Cape Argus, The. 1875. 27 November.

Cape Argus, The. 1899. 21 April

Cape Standard, The. 1945. 13 February.

Cape Times, The. 1897. 20 January.

Cape Times, The. 1898. 25 October.

Cape Times, The. 1899. 22 April.

Cleophas, F.J. & Van der Merwe, F.J.G. 2010a. The African Political Organisation's contribution to South African sport, 1909–1914. *African Journal for Physical, Health Education, Recreation and Dance (AJPHERD)*, 16(1):159–177.

Cleophas, F.J. & Van der Merwe, F.J.G. 2010b. The African Political Organisation's contribution to South African sport, 1909–1914. *African Journal for Physical, Health Education, Recreation and Dance (AJPHERD)*, 16(4):624–625.

Cleophas, F.J. 2011. Restarting the games: The African People's Organisation's contribution to South African sports in 1919 (Part III). *African Journal for Physical, Health Education, Recreation and Dance (AJPHERD)*, 17(4):708-719.

Cleophas, F.J. & Van der Merwe F.J.G. 2012. Exercising race through the Coronation Physical Training Competition. *South African Journal for Research in Sport, Physical Education and Recreation (SAJRSPER)*, 34(1):43-56.

Cleophas, F.J. 2013a. The African Political Organisation's contribution to South African sport in 1919. Part IV. *African Journal for Physical, Health Education, Recreation and Dance (AJPHERD)*, 19(1):193-205.

Cleophas, F.J. 2013b. Running a history programme outside the classroom. A case study of athletics at Zonnebloem College. *Yesterday & Today*, 8:63-87.

Cleophas, F.J. 2014. Opening a window on early twentieth century school sport in CapeTown society. *The International Journal of the History of Sport*, 31(15):1868–1881. https://doi.org/10.1080/09523367.2014.934679

Cleophas, F.J. 2015. The contribution of the African People's Organisation to sport in South Africa: July to December 1920. *African Journal for Physical, Health Education, Recreation and Dance (AJPHERD)*, 21(1:2):444–456.

Coghlan, D.V. 1986. The development of athletics in South Africa: 1814 to 1914. Volumes I and II. Unpublished PhD thesis. Grahamstown: Rhodes University.

Cradock Register, The. 1873. 30 May.

Difford, I. 1920. *The story of the 1st Cape Corps, 1915–1919*. Cape Town: Horter's Limited.

Du Toit, S.J. 1942. *Atletiek op ons skole*. Cape Town: Nasionale Pers Beperk.

Harrison, W. 194?. *Memoirs of a socialist in South Africa*. Cape Town: Harrison.

Hodgson, J. 1975. A history of Zonnebloem College 1858 to 1870, a study of church and society. Unpublished Master's thesis. Cape Town: University of Cape Town.

Le Roux, G. 1984. *90 Golden years*. Pretoria: South African Amateur Athletic Union.

Lewis, G. 1987. *Between the wire and the wall. A history of South African 'Coloured' politics*. New York: St. Martin's Press.

Muller, C.F.J. 1974. *Die oorsprong van die Groot Trek*. Cape Town: Tafelberg Publishers.

Odendaal, A. 2003. *The story of an African game. Black Cricketers and the Unmasking of One of South Africa's Greatest Myths, 1850–2003*. Cape Town: David Phillip Publishers.

Odendaal, A. 2017. Reflections on writing a post-colonial history of a colonial game. Decolonising Sport Historical Themes. Unpublished keynote address. Stellenbosch: Stellenbosch University Museum. 15–16 September.

Parker, G.A. 1897. *South African Sports*. London: Sampson Low, Marston.

SA Clarion, 1919a. 3 May.

SA Clarion, 1919b. 10 May.

SA Clarion, 1919c. 21 June.

SA Clarion, 1919d. 16 August.

SA Clarion, 1919e. 20 September.

SA Clarion, 1919f. 11 October.

SA Clarion, 1919g. 22 November.

SA Clarion, 1920a. 15 May.

SA Clarion, 1920b. 24 July.

SA Clarion, 1920c. 2 October.

SA Clarion, 1920d. 30 October.

SA Clarion, 1920e. 11 December.

SA Clarion, 1920f. 25 December.

Sleigh, D. 1973. *'n Man om te hardloop*. Cape Town: Tafelberg Publishers.

South African Spectator, 1901. 24 August.

South African Spectator, 1902. 25 January.

South African Spectator, 1902. 19 July.

Springboks ... past and present: a record of men and women who represented South Africa in international amateur sport, 1888-1947. 1947. Pietermaritzburg: South African Olympic and British Empire Games Association.

Steyn, D. 2015. *History of South African cross-country, middle- and long-distance running and walking - 1894 to 2014.* Volume 1 - 1894 to 1966. Villeria: Dewald Steyn.

Sun, The. 1934. 6 July.

Vamplew, W. 2013. Theories and typologies: A historical exploration of the Sports club in Britain. *The International Journal of the History of Sport,* 30(14). https://doi.org/10.1080/09523367.2013.817991

Vamplew, W. 2016. Playing together: towards a theory of the British sports club in history, *Sport in Society*, 19(3):455–469. https://doi.org/10.1080/17430437.2015.1062268

Van der Merwe, F.J.G. 1987. Britse invloed op atletiek in die Wes-Kaap. Unpublished M.A. thesis. Stellenbosch: Stellenbosch University.

Van der Merwe, F.J.G. 2007. *Sport history. A textbook for South African students.* Stellenbosch: F.J.G. Publications.

Van der Merwe, F.J.G. & Venter, C. 1987. Athletics as an indicator of the influence of British imperialism at the Cape. *South African Journal for Research in Sport, Physical Education and Recreation,* 10(2):73–82.

Van der Ross, R.E. 1975. *The Founding of the African People's Organisation in Cape Town in 1903 and the Role of Dr Abdurahman.* Pasadena: California Institute of Technology.

Van der Ross, R.E. 1986. *The rise and decline of Apartheid: A study of political movements among the Coloured people of South Africa, 1880-1985.* Cape Town: Tafelberg Publishers.

Vogt, W.H. 1951. Early athletics and cycling in South Africa. *Vigor,* 4(2):37–39.

Volksblad Het. 1873. 31 Mei.

Western Cape Archives and Records Services. MOOC 6/9/10596/ 89801.

Western Cape Archives and Records Services, MOOC 6/9/4782/50732.

Western Cape Archives and Records Services, MOOC 6/9/ 4776/ 50546.

Muslim women and sport: On traversing the politics of 'religious' identity

Nuraan Davids

Associate Professor, Education Policy Studies, Faculty of Education, Stellenbosch University

The theological centrality of Muslim women in and for Islam

Qur'anic exegeses reveal that issues of dress code, inheritance, marriage, divorce, sexuality, purity and modesty in Islam are all couched in the debates surrounding Muslim women. In turn, these debates, as Stowasser (1994:5) observes, are considered as central to the preservation and maintenance of Islamic "indigenous values". Traditionally, in her roles as wife and mother, declares Stowasser (1994:7), "the woman fights a holy war for the sake of Islamic values where her conduct, domesticity, and dress are vital for the survival of the Islamic way of life. Religion, morality, and culture stand and fall with her." In this sense, it is Muslim women who preserve the family, and hence, Islamic society. Consequently, while the Qur'an affords unprecedented rights – against a background of a highly patriarchal Arabian society – in terms of inheritance, marriage and divorce, these rights are not extended into dominant Muslim discourses. For example, particular historical accounts describe women of the first Muslim community as active participants in their faith and other social matters (Ahmed 1992:72). They are described as freely studying with men and other women – both in the *halaqāt* (study circles) and the madrassah (college). And after receiving their *ijāzāt* (certificates), they would continue to teach both men and women – bringing into contention the traditionally held view of sexually segregated spaces (Afsaruddin 2005:164).

Reports of Muslim women's involvement and engagement in relation to the historical unfolding of Islam, however, are not evident in dominant narratives on Islamic education. To a very large extent, as Afsaruddin (2005:163) argues, the historical influence and roles of Muslim women have been minimised. For this reason, Wadud (2006:77) is especially critical of religious sources. She maintains that the patriarchal actions among Muslims not only raise questions about the textual interpretations of the historical role and influence of Muslim women, but bring into contestation the content of particular religious sources. She argues that "interpretations of the textual sources, applications of those interpretations when constructing laws to govern personal and private Islamic affairs and to construct public policies and institutions to control Islamic policies and authority, are based upon male interpretive privilege" (Wadud 2006:22). As pointed out by Wadud (2002), there are more passages in the Qur'an that address issues pertaining to women, as individuals, as part of a family and as members of a community, than all the other issues combined. These passages, according to Stowasser (1994:21), are underscored by a recurrent message that "women's faith and righteousness are dependent on her own will and decision-making..."

Following on the above, Ramadan (2001:56) contends that the prioritisation of the family to Muslim women neither implies a relegation to the privacy of the family home, nor a passive compliance with regard to their faith. To this end, Muslim women are not expected to be exclusively occupied with matters related to the family or home. Both Qur'anic exegeses and historical records reveal and affirm that whatever expectations are placed on men, are equally placed on women. Barazangi (2000:24) clarifies that exploring the role of woman as a human entity in the Qur'an "does not merely concern a Muslim woman's freedom of speech and sexuality, or access to balanced education; it concerns woman as an autonomous spiritual and intellectual human being who will effect a change in history". It is therefore unsurprising, states Ramadan (2001:57–58), to find Muslim women who "defend both access to modernity and the principles of their religious and cultural practices at one and the same time. They are 'modern' without being 'Western'".

Muslim women and sport: a public/private debate?

Martin (2000) has combined the terms 'black' and 'woman' - forming "blackwoman" - in order to show the connection between race and gender. Similarly, Sherman (2005) has combined the terms 'black' and 'American' - forming "blackamerican" - to show the connection between race and citizenship. Following suit, Cooke (2008:91) constructs the neologism "Muslimwoman" to illustrate how the veil, real or imagined, functions like race, a marker of essential difference, which Muslim women seemingly cannot escape. Muslimwoman, explains Cooke (2008:91), draws attention to the emergence of a new, singular religious and gendered identification that overlays national, ethnic, cultural, historical and even philosophical diversity. She continues that "Muslim women are outsider/insiders within Muslim communities where, to belong, their identity increasingly is tied to the idea of the veil. As Muslims, they are negotiating cultural outsider/insider roles in Muslim-minority societies" (Cooke, 2008:91). In this regard, the challenge for Muslim women, and the reason they continue to be excluded and marginalised, according to Wadud (2006:8), is twofold. On the one hand, Muslim men assume and maintain authority, based on their own particular male interpretations of the sources (the Qur'an and the Sunnah). On the other hand, says Wadud, the conception of the public domain of an Islamic paradigm still focuses upon a fixed centre in public space as predominantly defined and inhabited by men.

Adding to the complexity of the public/private debate is that Muslim women have different ideas as to how this debate ought to be traversed - which are influenced by the extent (if any) to which an Islamic framework is allowed to enter the debate. Islamic feminism, for instance, locates Islam as central to its construction and discourse. This is unlike Western feminism, which has been largely secular, and hence, constructed outside of religious frameworks (Badran, 2009:2). Islamic feminism does not locate the spheres of public and private on opposite ends of a continuum. Instead, Badran (2009) explains, by supporting an egalitarian model of both family and society, Islamic feminists promote a more flowing public–private continuum of gender equality. This continuum discards the public–private division.

When this continuum is applied to the arena of Muslim women in sports, Islamic feminists seek to incorporate their Islamic identity into their roles as participants in sport. In other words, they seek to operate within an Islamic framework; they refer to the Qur'an as support for their demand of equal opportunity for girls and women in sports and society (Benn, Pfister & Jawad 2010:40). As such, explain Benn et al. (2010:40) "they believe that equal opportunity in sports is compatible with the traditional Islamic rules with respect to 'modest clothes' and/or segregation of the genders". By contrast, secular (sport) feminists, continue Benn et al. (2010:40), "demand a separation of state and religion; they opt for freedom of choice with respect to religion and lifestyle and demand that women be given the same access as men to all parts of society, including sports". There is yet another view held by Islamic feminists, who, like secular feminists, demand equal access and opportunities, but neither accept the arguments for gender segregation, nor the necessity of wearing the hijāb. In this regard, this view maintains that there are no religious rules which prohibit or regulate dress codes in order for Muslim women to participate in sports (Benn et al. 2010:40).

The contestation around access to the public domain is neither new nor unusual. Benhabib (1992) explains that access to the public sphere has always been curtailed by issues of race, class, gender and religion, as well as money and power. But she also states that religion, and religious identity, as a value system, presents one vehicle through which the problems of individualism, egotism and alienation in modern societies can be recovered. She refers to this as the "integrationist strain", which is in contrast to the "participatory strain", which ascribes the dilemmas of modernity more to a loss of a sense of political agency and efficacy than to a loss of belonging and unity. Benhabib (1992:77–78) elaborates that this loss of political agency is not as a result of the disconnection between the political and the personal, but rather as a result of two possibilities. One is the incongruity between the various spheres which reduces one's possibilities for agency in one sphere on the basis of one's position in another sphere. The second possibility is the fact that belonging in the various spheres effectively becomes exclusive due to the nature of the activities involved, while the mutual exclusivity of the spheres is fortified by the system. To Benhabib (1992:78–79), mere participation is not enough to solve the problems of modern identity and estrangement. Instead, she argues that what is required is not reconciliation, but political agency in the form of engagement. Active participation and belonging, states Waghid (2010:20), "are both conceptually connected to some form of engagement in relation to someone else – I participate with others in a conversation, so I engage with them; and I belong to a group where members are in conversation, so I engage with them by being attached to the conversation." Meaning, therefore, can only be produced when there is another, in the same way that cultures, says Benhabib (2002), are formed through dialogues with other cultures. In the absence, therefore, of engagement, active participation and belonging, Muslim women in modern societies are unable to produce meaning in those societies, and are prevented from forming new types of communities.

Hargreaves (2000:52) asserts that what lies at the heart of attitudes to women's sport in the Muslim world is that the "social construction of women in Islam is linked to the power of symbol and control over the body". In this sense, the female body in Islam "is at the centre of cultural contest, scrutiny and meaning, and Muslim women in sport encapsulate this contest" (*ibid*, 2000:53). As a result, we find, that although the Qur'anic concept of modesty applies to both men and women, in practice it has been used almost exclusively to regulate the attitudes to, and usage of women's bodies (*ibid*, 2000:52). Ironically, inasmuch as Western society criticises Islam for its perceived insistence on a dress code for Muslim women, liberal democracies might need to reflect on its own treatment of Muslim women. In an attempt to regulate the dress code in the public space, specifically of Muslim women, a number of liberal democracies have adopted increasingly narrow and restrictive regulations – effectively, prohibiting Muslim women from dressing how they choose to dress. As described by Hargreaves (2000:53), "The veil is a symbol of cultural difference. For non-Muslims it conveys the idea that Western women are liberated, and Muslim women, by comparison, are oppressed. The veil represents the 'Otherness' of Islam and is condemned in the West as a constricting mode of dress, a form of social control, and a religious sanctioning of women's invisibility and subordinate socio-political status".

Indeed, as Mahmood (2009:70) contends, much of the conflict surrounding the *hijāb* is because of an "impoverished understanding of images and signs, rather than paying attention to the embodied practice which informs a particular image or sign". Reducing the *hijāb* to a scrap of cloth, which Muslim men have imposed on Muslim women (which is how it is most commonly understood), according to Mernissl (1995:95), is to drain it of its meaning. Wearing the *hijāb* is an expression of the spiritual and sacred dimension of being. To Ramadan (2001:55-56) the reductionist interpretation of the *hijāb* hinders a coherent understanding of its meaning. He expounds that at a social level the *hijāb* is an expression of the spiritual and sacred dimension of being. To him, "It is about expressing, in our social life, that we are not body, that our worth is not in our forms and that our dignity lies in respect of our being and not in the visibility of our appeals and seductions" (Ramadan 2001:55-56).

Against the background of the afore-mentioned discussion, in the rest of this chapter, I will pay particular attention to the much publicised "Nike Pro hijab". Of particular concern is how its surrounding controversy is yet another instance of the contestation which Muslim women encounter as they traverse the public space of sport.

'Nike Pro hijāb', Muslim women, and the public discourse

Women's bodies, as Benhabib (2011:168) informs us, have become the site of symbolic confrontations between a re-essentialised understanding of religious and cultural differences and the forces of state power, whether in their civic-republican, liberal-democratic or multicultural form. One of the main reasons for the emergence of these confrontations or public debates, says Benhabib (2011:169), is because of the actual location of "political theology". She asserts that within the context of globalisation, the concept of "political theology" is complicated by its unstable location between religion and the public square; between the private and official; and between individual rights to freedom of religion versus state security and public well-being. Ultimately, therefore, the nature of the tension between religion as a "political theology" and the forces of state power can at best be described as a clash between identities of a collective nature (as envisaged by the nation-state) and identities of an individual nature (as manifested in different religions and cultures). The obvious visibility of a *hijāb*-clad Muslim woman places her at the heart of this clash. What liberal democracies demand of her is to de-veil, so that she might become less visible, and hence, publicly acceptable.

The decision, therefore, by Nike, to launch the "Nike Pro *hijāb*" comes as a predictable surprise. Predictable, because it makes business sense to follow a trend – already set by high-end designer names, such as Oscar de la Renta, Dolce and Gabbana, Versace, and DKNY – and tap into a formerly untraversed market of Muslim money, epitomised by the wealth found in the Gulf region. In this regard, Nike's latest attire has been dismissed as nothing else but opportunistic. Surprising, because it seemingly goes against the agenda of most liberal democracies to expunge the *hijāb* from their societies.

Nike's decision to introduce the Pro *hijāb* is motivated by their signature addendum: 'If you have a body, you're an athlete.' https://www.nike.com/us/en_us/c/women/nike-pro-hijab

Although welcomed by some (mostly Muslim women), most of, and the harshest criticism, has come from those who have condemned the "Nike Pro *hijāb*" as an endorsement of the oppression of women. Criticism on social media, like the examples below, have promoted tweets of dissent with the hashtag #BoycottNike:

"#Nike cashing in on the subjugation, domination, and oppression of women."

"@Nike has decided to capitalize off Islamic patriarchy by putting their brand on a chastity helmet."

"I will never buy another Nike product again."

"Congratulations, @Nike, for normalizing the oppression of women through the Pro Hijab. Disgusting."

Drowning in the above discontent, however, are three significant facts and factors. Firstly, the participation of Muslim women in sport is not new. Secondly, Muslim women who participate in sport, and who wish to maintain an Islamic dress code – as in wearing the *hijāb* – have done so. Thirdly, the impression that Nike is the first to promote a *hijāb*, specifically geared towards athletes, is misplaced. The first person to design and market a "performance-oriented *hijab*" or "athletic *hijab*", is Dutch designer, Cindy van den Bremen, in 1999. Today, her company, Capsters, sells eight styles via its site. Nike's introduction of the "Pro *hijāb*", therefore, is not a ground-breaking endeavour – regardless of what their campaign might infer:

The Nike Pro Hijab has been a year in the making, but its impetus can be traced much further back to Nike's founding mission, to serve athletes, with the signature addendum: If you have a body, you're an athlete... As each country has its own particular hijab style, the ideal design would need to accommodate variances. The brand also solicited the opinions of advocates and local communities to ensure the design met cultural requirements... By providing Muslim athletes with the most groundbreaking products, like the Nike Pro Hijab, Nike aims to serve

51

today's pioneers as well as inspire even more women and girls in the region who still face barriers and limited access to sport... (Nike Pro Hijab. Nike.com)

Seemingly, due to its global recognition, what the "Nike Pro *hijāb*" campaign has put into motion is to mainstream what is generally considered as a marginalised and marginalising garment. Within a context of intensifying levels of Islamophobia, increasingly directed at Muslim women, it is inconceivable that Nike would not have expected the inevitable political and social backlash. While one might argue and dismiss Nike's primary motivation as making business sense, the political insinuations of its "Pro *hijāb*" should not be undermined. What Nike—perhaps inadvertently—has done, is to legitimise the *hijāb* across two very different narratives: one in response to hostile liberal democracies that are adamant in modernising Muslim women, by stripping them of their *hijāb*. And the other in response to normative constructions of Islam, which might consider the traditional dress and role of Muslim women as irreconcilable with the modern arena of sport. However, the latter argument raises a number of complex questions. These include: Why might it be necessary for a Western global brand to legitimise the wearing of the *hijāb* in sport? To what extent might we interpret the "Nike Pro *hijāb*" as a commentary on the public/private debate and controversies that have thus far dominated the wearing of the *hijāb* in liberal democracies? So, what is Nike selling and marketing – the hijāb or the controversy?

Religious identity as controversy?

There is no doubt that, particularly in Muslim countries, sport is providing an avenue through which Muslim women might not only participate in the public domain, but also participate in their own citizenship as women. As evident as the visibility of Muslim women in sport might be, what is not so evident is the tension between the modern nation state and how Muslim women navigate their way through this terrain, while remaining attached to their religious identities as a physical manifestation. The manner in which secularism and the modern state have chosen to address Muslim women, who wear the *hijāb*, explains Davids (2014:308), does not demonstrate any understanding of the practice itself. She continues that to treat it merely as a symbol of something else – namely oppression and backwardness – highlights the serious misrecognition of Muslim women. And, one cannot ignore the possibility that, like those modern nation states, who have chosen to vilify the *hijāb* as a symbol of oppression, and hence irreconcilable with a democratic public sphere, Nike, too, has jumped onto the bandwagon of engaging with the *hijāb* as a symbol, rather than as enactment of religious identity. In other words, as Mirza (2013:305) asserts, "The Muslim woman's private faith-based reasons for wearing the niqab have become public property, a 'weapon' used by many different competing interests, from male politicians in France to white feminists in Belgium to argue their cases for and against assimilation, multiculturalism, secularism and human rights." At the core of these regulations, states Mirza (2013:305) are moves to enframe constructions of acceptable public dress, and hence identity.

What is necessary, therefore, to counter the symbolic treatment of the *hijāb,* and hence, Muslim women? What is needed for Muslim women to enter the public arena - whether it is the sport arena or the public square - as equals, rather than a symbol or image that needs to be tolerated? Unless Muslim women are afforded the same degrees of inclusion - based on practices of deliberative engagement - they will continue to stand on the periphery not only of their respective political communities, but on the edge of their own identities. Habermas (2008), for example, insists that the equal inclusion of all citizens requires not only a political culture that preserves liberal attitudes from being confused with indifference, but that inclusion can only be achieved in a society in which equal citizenship, and cultural and religious difference complement each other in the right way. Consequently, it should be up to Muslim women to decide how, when and where to enact their identities as Muslim women, and if the *hijāb* is one embodiment of this identity, then the decision to wear it should not be left to the discretion or mercy of liberal democracies. It is the decision of Muslim women to decide the parameters of how they engage their respective identities with the public sphere, and these parameters should neither be infringed upon though coercion (as in certain Muslim-majority states), nor through regulation (as in certain liberal democracies). Inasmuch therefore as certain Muslim women, and others, might welcome the "Nike Pro *hijāb*", how Muslim women, as well as other religious groups, decide to self-identify, and participate in the public sphere, belongs to the individual, rather than to the social, or in this case, a sporting conglomerate.

References

Afsaruddin, A. 2005. Muslim Views on Education: Parameters, Purview, and Possibilities. *Journal of Catholic Legal Studies*, 44(143):143–178.

Ahmed, L. 1992. *Women and Gender in Islam: Historical Roots of a Modern Debate*. New Haven, CT: Yale University Press.

Badran, M. 2009. *Feminism in Islam: Secular and Religious Convergences*. Oxford: Oneworld.

Barazangi, N.H. 2000. Muslim Women's Islamic Higher Learning as a Human Right. In G. Webb (ed.). *Windows of Faith*. NY: Syracuse University Press. 22–47.

Benhabib, S. 1992: *Situating the self: gender, community and postmodernism in contemporary ethics*. UK: Polity Press.

Benhabib, S. 2002. *The claims of culture: equality and diversity in the global era*. Princeton, New Jersey: Princeton University Press.

Benhabib, S. 2011. *Dignity in adversity: human rights in troubled times*. UK: Polity Press.

Benn, T., Pfister, G. & Jawad, H. 2010. *Muslim women and sport*. New York & London: Routledge. https://doi.org/10.4324/9780203880630

Cooke, M. 2008. Deploying the Muslim woman. *Journal of Feminist Studies in Religion,* 24(1):91–99. https://doi.org/10.2979/FSR.2008.24.1.91

Davids, N. 2014. Muslim women and the politics of religious identity in a (post) secular society. *Studies in Philosophy of Education,* 33(3):303–313. https://doi.org/10.1007/s11217-013-9389-9

Habermas, J. 2008. Notes on a post-secular society. http://www.signandsight.com/features/1714.html [Accessed 4th February 2017].

Hargreaves, J. 2000. *Heroines of sport: The politics of difference and identity*. Routledge: London & New York.

Martin, J.M. 2000. *More than Chains and Toil: A Christian Work Ethic of Enslaved Women*. Louisville, KY: Westminster John Knox Press.

Mernissi, F. 1995. *Women and Islam: an historical and theological enquiry*. UK: Blackwell Publishers.

Mirza, H.S. 2013. Embodying the veil: Muslim women and gendered Islamophobia in 'New Times'. In Z. Gross, L. Davies, & D. Al-Khansaa (eds.). *Gender, religion and education in a chaotic postmodern world.* Dordrecht: Springer. 303–318. https://doi.org/10.1007/978-94-007-5270-2_20

Nike Pro Hijab. Nike.com. https://www.nike.com/us/en_us/c/women/nike-pro-hijab. [Accessed 4th July 2017].

Ramadan, T. 2001. *Islam, the West and the challenges of modernity.* UK: The Islamic Foundation.

Sherman, J. 2005. *Islam and the Blackamerican: Looking toward the Third Resurrection.* New York: Oxford University Press.

Stowasser, B. 1994. *Women in the Qur'an, Traditions and Interpretations.* New York: Oxford University Press.

Wadud, A. 2002. A'ishah's Legacy. *New Internationalist Magazine,* 345(1). http://newint. org/features/2002/05/01/aishahs-legacy/. [Accessed 4th February 2017].

Wadud, A. 2006. *Inside the Gender Jihad: Women's Reform in Islam.* Oxford: Oneworld.

Waghid, Y. 2010: *Education, democracy and citizenship revisited: pedagogical encounters.* AFRICAN SUN MeDIA: Stellenbosch.

Discord in the dressing room: The ideological complexities within non-racial football during the late 1970s

Gustav Venter
Research Coordinator, Centre for Human Performance Sciences, Stellenbosch University

Introduction

The body of academic literature on South African football has grown steadily over the past decade, largely as a result of the country's hosting of the 2010 FIFA World Cup. Works by, for example, Alegi and Bolsmann (2010a & 2010b), Bolsmann (2013) and Darby (2008) constitute merely a small sample of many such studies. Despite this development, fertile ground for further exploration remains. This includes the internal dynamics of the non-racial sport movement, particularly as it related to football. It is this latter aspect with which this chapter is concerned. By using the 1978 professional football season as a case study, it endeavours to highlight the internal complexities which were at the time prevalent within the non-racial movement broadly, and within non-racial football specifically. These are important considerations when reflecting upon the ideological stance of the South African Council on Sport (SACOS) and the practical implications this had for some of its member bodies such as the South African Soccer Federation (SASF) and its professional league, the Federation Professional League (FPL). Ironically it was developments relating to clubs formerly within the SASF's ideological enemy, namely the whites-only National Football League (NFL), which ultimately brought some of these internal disagreements to the fore during the course of 1978. It is argued that this chain of events serves as a marker of the tension between ideological and practical concerns – an important historical consideration when reflecting upon the approach followed by the non-racial sport movement during this period.

Surveying the football landscape: An overview

During the 1970s South Africa had three professional football leagues operating concurrently within widely differing ideological contexts. The oldest was the whites-only National Football League (NFL), formed in 1959, and operating under the auspices of the white controlling body, the Football Association of South Africa (FASA). The largest league was the National Professional Soccer League (NPSL) which represented the professional arm of the South African National Football Association (SANFA), for Africans. Both these leagues operated within government structures and adhered to the apartheid practice of playing sport separately among South Africa's race groups.[1] Opposed to this was the non-racial Federation Professional League (FPL) which rejected the idea of racial classification and played sport on an integrated basis outside formal government structures. This was the professional arm of the non-racial SASF, which was in turn affiliated to SACOS.

During the course of the 1970s the NFL found itself within a drastically changing football landscape while simultaneously experiencing various economic and operational pressures. Venter (2015) has recently dealt with the latter as well as the former (2017). These factors led to the league folding after the 1977 season, thereby leaving its clubs without a league structure to participate in. This left former NFL clubs with the choice of joining either the NPSL or the FPL. The latter was, of course, already being played on an integrated basis outside formal structures, while the former was permitted to integrate on account of the government's evolving sports policy at the time. The geographic position of clubs was a significant factor that dictated the outcome of this process, since clubs preferred to join a league that would result in reduced travel costs. In this regard five former NFL clubs – four of which were based at the coast – threw in their lot with the FPL during 1978. This was no coincidence since the majority of existing FPL clubs were situated along South Africa's coastal belt. This development offers a rare example of white sports teams migrating from formal government structures into the opposing non-racial camp. This resulted in a series of ideological and practical complications which constitute the central subject of this analysis.

A flirtation with non-racialism: Former NFL clubs join the FPL

By the time the 1978 league programme was set to commence the FPL boasted five clubs from the previous season's NFL first division. These were Durban City, Hellenic, Cape Town City, East London United and Roodepoort Guild – the latter being the only Transvaal-based club in the group. Two other NFL clubs had since been taken over by existing FPL clubs – Durban United was merged with Verulam Suburbs under the chairmanship of the latter's Errol Vawda, while Maritzburg was acquired by Durban-based Berea (*South African Soccer* February 1978:17). This was an indication of the challenging economic circumstances experienced by NFL clubs during the preceding years. The FPL also included one former NPSL club, namely Wanderers – a break-away group from African Wanderers (which continued in the NPSL). This resulted in the FPL fielding a seventeen-team first division in 1978 – an appreciable increase from the eleven teams the year before (*South African Soccer* April 1978:6).

Such an arrangement was bound to present logistical and financial challenges – and this proved to be the case. Clubs were forced to undertake extended fixture programmes and increased travel distances compared to previous seasons – whether they were existing FPL members or former NFL clubs. The FPL treasurer, Bobby Naicker, released the respective travel budgets for the competing teams, with the four Cape Town-based sides (which included Cape Town City and Hellenic) incurring the greatest cost. The estimated total cost of long-distance air travel (excluding accommodation) for these clubs during the league

---

1   The Population Registration Act of 1950 classified South African citizens into four racial groups, namely African, coloured, Indian and white.

season amounted to R21,000 each – 40% more than the estimated amount of R15,000 for each of the six Natal-based clubs (*South African Soccer* April 1978:11).

As a reference point Cape Town City's actual expenditure on air travel during the 1976 and 1977 NFL seasons amounted to R15,480 and R24,600 respectively. However, these figures included accommodation as well as travel for away matches in cup competitions (*Cape Town City Football Club Income Statement* 31 October 1977). The 1978 FPL estimates were for league matches only and excluded accommodation. The fact that these latter elements represented additional costs that still had to be factored in is an indication as to the potential financial predicament facing FPL clubs. This was especially true in the case of Cape Town City, particularly given the club's struggles over the preceding years. Teams from the Transvaal were better off, with projected spending of R16,750 on long-distance travel, while costs for the East London and Port Elizabeth-based clubs were projected to be around R18,750 and R20,000 respectively. However, compared to the rival NPSL, the FPL clubs faced a more challenging travel schedule irrespective of their geographic location. In this regard the 1978 NPSL first division did not contain any teams from Cape Town, Port Elizabeth or East London, meaning that competing teams faced fewer long-distance trips. Transvaal-based teams in the NPSL, for example, faced a maximum of five long-distance trips during the 1978 league season, whereas their counterparts in the FPL faced twelve such journeys (*South African Soccer* April 1978:11). These figures serve to highlight some of the practical issues confronting clubs within this new context.

Professional football and ideology: Pressure from SACOS

In addition to the potential financial challenges faced by clubs it is also important to bear in mind the ideological context within which the FPL operated. The fact that the league represented the professional arm of the non-racial SASF – which in turn was affiliated to SACOS – had notable ramifications. In April 1977 SACOS adopted the following stance known as the double-standards resolution:

> Any person, whether he is a player, an administrator or a spectator, committed to the non-racial principle in sport, shall not participate in or be associated with any other codes of sport which practice, perpetuate or condone racialism or multi-nationalism. Players and/or administrators disregarding the essence of this principle shall be guilty of practicing [*sic*] double-standards, and cannot therefore, be members of any organisation affiliated to SACOS! (*SACOS Statement* 6 April 1977)

This far-reaching resolution encapsulated SACOS's strategy of complete non-collaboration with government-backed structures from that point onwards. It had a significant impact on some SACOS members, including the SASF and FPL. In this regard the FPL received a gently worded warning from SACOS secretary, M.N. Pather, early in 1978 in the form of a letter to be read at the FPL's annual general meeting. It stated in part:

> We wish you well and sincerely hope that in the ensuing year you will not tolerate racialism of any kind nor will you entertain double standards. In this regard you accepted our directive [the double-standards resolution]…We believe you will implement this directive as it will not only enhance your status but will give it the credibility we seek (*Minutes of SACOS General Meeting* 5 March 1978:7).

This exchange is recounted in the minutes of a SACOS general meeting held on 5 March 1978, and it is revealing that the minutes specifically also indicate that the aforementioned letter was not read at the earlier FPL general meeting as intended. Apparently Abdul Bhamjee, the public relations officer of the SASF at the time, "was quick to say that the letter would be read at the next Management Committee meeting of the [Federation] Pro League" (*Minutes of SACOS General Meeting* 5 March 1978:7–8). This is perhaps indicative of mounting tension between the SASF and SACOS at the time, particularly in light of developments over the preceding months.

This included Bhamjee and SASF president, Norman Middleton, meeting with FASA leadership on 30 September 1977 to discuss the latter's proposed incorporation into the SASF (*Minutes of FASA Executive Committee Meeting* 30 September 1977:1). Further talks ensued in the subsequent months, while on the professional side former NFL clubs were joining the FPL of their own accord. It also has to be remembered that Middleton resigned as SACOS president early in 1977 due to pressure within his own ranks regarding his affiliation to the Coloured People's Representative Council – a government structure. In light of the double-standards resolution the aforementioned developments were not viewed favourably by some SACOS members.

This gave rise to a heated exchange during the SACOS general meeting on 5 March 1978 which reveals the complex set of circumstances created by the double-standards resolution. The exchange began with Middleton objecting to a recent distribution of pamphlets by provincial Councils of Sport (SACOS's provincial units) calling for a boycott on professional football. This related to unhappiness felt in some quarters regarding the FPL's "linking up" with former NFL clubs during this period – apparently without the consultation of "local clubs" (*Minutes of SACOS General Meeting* 5 March 1978:16). The preceding month also saw the staging of a pre-season tournament sponsored by Castle Lager contested between the four Cape Town-based FPL sides (Cape Town City, Hellenic, Cape Town Spurs and Glenville). In this regard one delegate opined that "token matches against white clubs are confusing to black players".

According to the minutes Middleton's response was that "we blacks don't know what to do with our freedom", and he reiterated that the SASF stood "firmly behind SACOS" and that it would "accept players of all shades whether they are black, white, pink or brown". Despite these exhortations he was accused by one delegate of "deliberately participating in the fraud of compromisation". The same delegate also stated that the SASF was "guilty of double standards", particularly with regard to permitting "Cape Town City to remain members of the white Western Province body, whilst it was an affiliate of the SASF". This related to the fact that Cape Town City utilised Hartleyvale – a stadium owned by the (white amateur) Western Province Football Association (WPFA) – as its home ground. Cape Town City's junior teams were also set to continue playing in WPFA leagues – a problematic arrangement in the eyes of SACOS which viewed anything other than immediate total integration at all levels as unacceptable.

Middleton in turn warned that "people in glass houses should not throw stones", and stated that people were "out of date with the term 'non-racialism'". Bhamjee rose to his support: "We are mistrusting one another. Our aims are the same but some only take different roads... The Federation has done a good job so far in denting the massive white privileged body." However Frank van der Horst, vice president of SACOS, entered the fray and took a hard line:

> [The] trouble began when the SASF began to have secret talks with the white officials. A former senior official of SACOS [Middleton] has flagrantly abused the principles of SACOS. Norman Middleton has sold out. The facts speak for themselves. Everyone can see the purpose of the merger and [the] Federation is rescuing the NFL. This whole development dovetails completely in with the present Multi-national policy. SACOS must not allow [the] Federation to continue with multi-nationalism.

In response Middleton demanded that SACOS "take a stand against the Federation", and as a result the following motion was unanimously carried:

> The General Council of SACOS views with alarm the fact that the SASF has [succumbed] to the multi-national policy of the Government and hereby calls on the SASF to show cause within six months why its membership and the membership of the Professional League with SACOS should not be terminated (*Minutes of SACOS General Meeting* 5 March 1978:16–18).

This exchange is a clear indication of the troubling position in which the SASF – and in particular its professional league, the FPL – found itself regarding the uncompromising SACOS framework. Upon reflection it is difficult to find any validity in SACOS's accusation that the SASF – by allowing former NFL teams into the FPL – was partaking in multinationalism.[2] After all, the league allowed the movement of players between the different clubs – something which was still against government policy at the time. It is argued here that this aggressive stance by SACOS was indicative of an atmosphere of suspicion which existed within the organisation during this period. In this regard Booth points out that while the double-standards resolution "was initially a strategy to build internal discipline", it "progressively became a tactic of political purification", and that "SACOS willingly sacrificed members and refused to consider alternative strategies" (Booth 1998:151-2). The SASF's membership of SACOS was terminated six months later on 15 October 1978 during a two-day general meeting of SACOS in which no SASF delegates were present (*Minutes of SACOS General Meeting* 14 October 1978:33).

It is revealing to consider the position of Cape Town City subsequent to the initial SACOS general meeting held on 5 March 1978. The club came under renewed pressure from the SASF to disassociate itself from the WPFA by 31 March – a clear outflow from the SASF discussions with SACOS. After playing only a handful of matches in the 1978 FPL league season the club dropped a bombshell on the football fraternity by announcing its withdrawal from the FPL in favour of the rival NPSL. It issued a brief statement partially clarifying the decision:

> The reason for this action is that we cannot accept the conditions of a directive issued to the club by the SASF as these would seriously prejudice the future of Cape Town City, our juniors, our supporters, and the association with the WP Football Association, and Hartleyvale (*Cape Times* 4 April 1978:16).

---

2   The government's multinational sport policy – which evolved since its inception in 1971 – by this time dictated that leagues could be racially mixed, but not the teams themselves. In other words, a league could contain "African" and "white" teams for example, but players from different racial groups could not play for the same team. Despite such racial mixing being contrary to government policy, it was technically not illegal and consequently teams ignored this provision from the late 1970s onwards.

The journalist André van der Zwan also speculated that meagre attendances at FPL league matches – even at that early stage of Cape Town City's league programme – prompted the club directors to make the switch: "The match against Maritzburg City [at Hartleyvale] drew only 1,100 spectators, but at the week end Mr Lewis [chairman], Mr Funston [director] and manager Frank Lord attended NPSL games in Soweto where crowds of 30,000 were recorded." The fact that the NPSL league programme for 1978 had already commenced by the time Cape Town City withdrew from the FPL meant that the club had to play a series of friendly encounters against NPSL clubs over the remainder of the season. The team was, however, promised a place in the NPSL first division for 1979 – the main drawcard – and was able to enter the 1978 Mainstay Cup competition (*South African Soccer* April 1978:27). The latter essentially constituted the premier knockout competition open to teams outside the non-racial SASF.

Cape Town City's decision to cross over to the NPSL naturally drew criticism from the SASF. Middleton warned other clubs to get out immediately "if they [had] similar motives", and he "lashed City for being more concerned about making money than fostering non-racial soccer". He also pointed out that the SASF "would not allow them to have two masters" (*South African Soccer* April 1978:27). There does appear to be notable inconsistency with regard to the application of this policy by the SASF – a scenario which brought further pressure from SACOS. Cape Town's other former NFL club, Hellenic, was able to continue in the FPL despite not severing all its ties with the white amateur body. According to chairman, Chris Christodolides, the Western Province Football Board (the SASF's non-racial affiliate in the province) "accepted that it would not be practical for our juniors and reserves to play in their leagues" (*Cape Times* 5 April 1978:20). During another SACOS general meeting, held a few months later, one of the delegates pointed out to the SASF that "the Junior Hellenic team was playing in FASA [the white national amateur body] but under another name" (*Minutes of SACOS General Meeting* 22 July 1978:21). It is worth noting that Hellenic's professional team played its FPL home matches at the Green Point Stadium – a venue that was not owned by the (white) Western Province Football Association, as was the case with Cape Town City's home ground, Hartleyvale. This possibly resulted in Hellenic's participation in the FPL being less contentious – from an SASF point of view – than that of Cape Town City.

Cape Town City's defection is an obvious indication that the original decision by former NFL clubs to join the FPL was certainly not driven by an overriding concern for playing principled, non-racial football. In this regard it is argued that there was a clear incompatibility between ideology and professionalism. During this period football was the only major sport code in South Africa also played in a professional form and this brought with it an additional layer of complications. It would have been, for example, far easier to take a principled stance on an issue such as sponsorship within an amateur environment where costs are greatly reduced due to the absence of player salaries. Professional football did not offer this luxury – both from a club and league perspective. The SASF and FPL offer clear examples of this.

Having lost its long-standing Mainstay league sponsorship in 1977, the FPL subsequently obtained a Castle Lager sponsorship from South African Breweries (SAB) for the 1978 FPL season. SAB already had an existing sponsorship relationship with the NPSL and therefore was able to corner the sponsorship market for professional football in South Africa by also investing in the FPL. The brewing behemoth's total sponsorship for the two leagues during 1978 amounted to R130,000, of which R75,000 went to the NPSL and R55,000 to the FPL (Alegi P & Bolsmann C 2010a:10). The decision by the SASF (and FPL) to move ahead with the SAB sponsorship came in for criticism from SACOS, as articulated by a Western Province delegate, Y. Ebrahim, in March 1978:

> ...the SASF should have consulted with all concerned before accepting sponsorship. This SASF promised to do before deciding. Whilst the SASF decried Stellenbosch Farmers' Winery's handout to the Football Council of SA [in 1977] and rejected its product, Mainstay, the SASF willingly accepted the sponsorship from the SA Breweries, after all Stellenbosch Farmers' Winery and SA Breweries are the one and the same people (*Minutes of SACOS General Meeting* 5 March 1978:17).

Setting the specific dispute regarding Mainstay aside, it is worth reflecting on the fact that during 1978 the FPL therefore shared the same title sponsor as the rival NPSL – the league which was still being characterised as "racial" and "multinational" in character by the non-racial movement. This betrays the fact that taking a principled stance – such as refusing the SAB sponsorship – would have been commendable in theory, but unrealistic in practice. The FPL, like the NPSL (and NFL previously), depended heavily on sponsorship for its survival, meaning that principled action could only be implemented up to a point.

This also applied to the league's clubs – including those that were long-standing FPL members. In this regard Pretoria-based Sundowns followed in Cape Town City's footsteps by also quitting the FPL for the NPSL during the early stages of the 1978 season. According to club secretary, Yusuf Mohamed, the main reason for the decision again related to finance. The prospect of a R20,000 air travel bill, coupled with low attendances and problems with regard to obtaining a home ground meant that "the club would never survive in the Federation Professional League" (*South African Soccer*, May 1978:14). Sundowns was undoubtedly not the only FPL club affected by the problematic situation that arose as a result of an enlarged league and increased air travel expenses. Later that year Swaraj – the defending FPL league champions from 1977 – signalled its intent to move to the NPSL in 1979. Shoukat Loonat, the club chairman, explained the reasoning in the press: "The soccer scene has become a battlefield and the fittest will survive. The FPL was, at one stage, better equipped. Now the NPSL is in the driving seat. Our survival depends on our playing in the NPSL" (*Rand Daily Mail* 19 October 1978).

To talk or not to talk: A split in the FPL

Throughout 1978 the issue of engaging in formal dialogue with the NPSL proved to be a controversial issue within SASF and FPL ranks. In fact, by the middle of the season there was a clear split among FPL clubs, with the Transvaal-based teams and former NFL clubs in particular favouring the idea of engaging in dialogue with NPSL representatives. This was to form part of a broader (and previously unsuccessful) effort to establish a single "Super League" in South Africa. During an FPL management committee meeting held in Durban on 20 August the majority of first division clubs (eight out of fifteen at the time) voted in favour of dialogue. These comprised the three Lenasia-based teams (Swaraj, Dynamos United and PG Bluebells United), the four remaining former NFL teams (Roodepoort Rangers, Durban City, East London United and Hellenic), as well as Maritzburg City from Natal (*South African Soccer* August 1978:13).

However, they were out-voted by the FPL executive and management committee members who were set against the idea of having talks with rival bodies. The reported vote count was 17–9. The nine votes in favour of dialogue comprised the eight clubs mentioned above as well as a vote by Abdul Bhamjee who was vice-president of the FPL at the time. This gave rise to frustration on the part of the professional clubs that were in favour of dialogue. From their point of view this was the majority opinion amongst the clubs, but could not be pursued since it was met by an intransigent block of votes from the executive opposing this course of action. This was seen as interference in the affairs of professional clubs by amateur officials.

According to FPL chairman, R.K. Naidoo, such dialogue would have constituted "a fraud", and he indicated that there would be no dialogue "until normal soccer starts at grass roots level". This was in line with SACOS's all-or-nothing approach and did not take into consideration the practical struggles experienced by clubs at ground level. Naidoo added that "he was not concerned even if [this approach] meant that the FPL will soon be without sponsorship" (*South African Soccer* August 1978:13). This view came in for heavy criticism in *South African Soccer* – a monthly football magazine which originally started as the FPL's own publication but which by 1978 included coverage of the NPSL as well.[3] In a sarcastically worded article in October 1978 it attacked Naidoo on various issues, including sponsorship: "You are not interested in sponsorship – how do you expect to run your league. Presumably with the support of the people...Try it Mr Naidoo, with the assistance of your executive and management committee" (*South African Soccer* October 1978:21).

This exchange is indicative of a rift between certain professional clubs on the one hand and some hard-line SASF/FPL officials on the other. The aforementioned criticism in *South African Soccer* essentially came from within the SASF itself since the publication fell under the auspices of Abdul Bhamjee. Bhamjee himself was a key figure in this dispute and sided with the clubs favouring dialogue with the NPSL. It is therefore not surprising to find his magazine directing criticism at Naidoo on this issue. During the heated meeting on 20 August Bhamjee was ordered out of the room by Naidoo, leading to a walk-out by delegates from the Transvaal-based FPL clubs in protest. These clubs subsequently demanded Naidoo's resignation and threatened to discontinue their 1978 league fixtures. This was only averted once Norman Middleton intervened to negotiate a temporary halt in hostilities a few days later.

South African Soccer further bemoaned these developments: "The character assassination, cliqueism [sic] and personality clashes are diseases that will continue to cloud the real issues confronting professional clubs, today" (*South African Soccer* August 1978:12-3). Events at the 20 August meeting also had further ramifications as Hellenic decided to quit the FPL the following day. The *Cape Times* reported that the club's management committee took this decision after chairman, Chris Christodolides, "had failed to get an assurance that the SASF would agree to dialogue with rival football organizations". The issue of dialogue was clearly a central consideration for many clubs, and it was even reported that "Hellenic demanded this assurance a few weeks [before the meeting] and suspended their fixtures trying to

---

3   The magazine originally came into being as *Fed Fan* in August 1976 under the editorship of Tanga Padayachee, although the project itself fell under the auspices of Abdul Bhamjee, the SASF's public relations officer. The magazine's name was changed to *Fed Fan Soccer* in June 1977 before finally adopting the name *South African Soccer* from February 1978 onwards. During 1978 the content reflected the dual nature of professional football in South Africa with coverage afforded to both Castle leagues (FPL and NPSL). Throughout this period Padayachee remained the editor. From 1979 onwards coverage shifted heavily towards the NPSL. Symbolically this reflected the dominant position which the NPSL had obtained by that time, but practically it was in line with Bhamjee's own estrangement from the SASF. He later joined the NPSL ranks as an influential official during the 1980s.

force a favourable answer" (*Cape Times* 22 August 1978:18). The club soon applied to the NPSL and was therefore placed on the same course as Cape Town City with the prospect of entering the league during the 1979 season.

Outcome of the 1978 season

The 1978 season was also characterised by unstable ownership of some FPL clubs. Swaraj was a notable example: "This club changed hands, and names, so often that the ordinary soccer follower became confused. At various stages it was known as Swaraj, Johannesburg Rangers, Johannesburg City, BP Swaraj, and then Swaraj again and towards the end, again Johannesburg City" (*South African Soccer* January 1979:10). These developments have to be viewed in the context of an enlarged seventeen-team league (initially) and the accompanying challenges regarding the financial sustainability of such a structure. By the end of the year clubs found themselves in an unpredictable, uncertain situation that somewhat resembled the final season of the NFL the year before. Many clubs were fighting for financial survival and took matters into their own hands, leaving the non-racial principle by the wayside. The issue of dialogue with the NPSL had been a contentious one throughout the year, causing a split within SASF ranks. Despite SACOS's warnings to the contrary – and an agreeable block of opinion within the SASF – Norman Middleton and Abdul Bhamjee reached out to NPSL officials behind the scenes. This incurred the wrath of SACOS:

> Although the SASF, at its recent Biennial General Meeting held at Cape Town resolved unanimously [not to pursue dialogue], the SASF President and its Public Relations Officer, were opting for dialogue and [newspaper] reports in this regard not only caused confusion but left soccer in a state of flux... [The] failure of SASF to discredit these press reports confirmed the viewpoint that there is a division in the Federation (*Minutes of SACOS General Meeting* 14 October 1978:28).

This development, coupled with other contentious points in the SASF-SACOS relationship, led to the termination of both the SASF and FPL's memberships with SACOS in October 1978. Within this milieu of uncertainty FPL clubs proceeded with dialogue on an individual basis and negotiated for openings in the 1979 NPSL first division. In light of the fact that – at an organisational level – no agreement was ultimately reached between the NPSL and SASF/FPL in terms of establishing a single league, the NPSL first division became the de facto "Super League" in South Africa. This came about by virtue of the defections by FPL clubs to the NPSL towards the end of 1978. The defectors included Dynamos, Bluebells, Swaraj, Cape Town Spurs, East London United and Suburbs United – all of which submitted applications to the NPSL for the 1979 season. This was of course in addition to the three teams – Cape Town City, Hellenic and Sundowns – which had already withdrawn from the SASF during the course of 1978 (*Rand Daily Mail,* 17 November 1978).

Conclusion

This chapter considered the brief foray of former (white) NFL teams into the non-racial FPL during the 1978 season as a window towards highlighting the complexities which existed within the non-racial sport movement at the time. The FPL and its parent body, the SASF, were positioned within a specific ideological context – a scenario that led to notable discontent within the league as a result of developments during 1978. The influence of SACOS was decisive in this regard as the latter's hard-line stance on dialogue (which it regarded as a form of collaboration) created a pressurised situation in which ideological outlook could no longer be reconciled with the realities of professional football. Coupled with the economic pressures faced by FPL clubs – largely as a result of increased travel costs – clubs were faced with a battle for survival. This ultimately gave rise to a split within the league with a number of teams defecting to the rival NPSL both during and after the season. This episode serves to illustrate the constant tension which existed between ideological and practical considerations as far as non-racial professional football was concerned. It is worth reflecting on this state of affairs when considering the broader landscape of anti-apartheid sport. A decade later South Africa began to move towards sporting unity – a chain of events that saw the non-racial movement being sidestepped largely on account of a dogmatic approach to aspects such as negotiation and compromise (Booth 2003). It is argued that the 1978 FPL season contained some notable antecedents for this process.

References

Alegi, P. & Bolsmann, C. 2010a. From Apartheid to Unity: White Capital and Black Power in the Racial Integration of South African Football, 1976–1992. *African Historical Review*, 42(1):1–18. https://doi.org/10.1080/17532523.2010.483783

Alegi, P. & Bolsmann, C. (eds.). 2010b. *South Africa and the Global Game: Football, Apartheid and Beyond.* London: Routledge.

Bolsmann, C. 2013. Professional Football in Apartheid South Africa: Leisure, Consumption and Identity in the National Football League, 1959–1977. *The International Journal of the History of Sport,* 30(16):1947–1961. https://doi.org/10.1080/09523367.2013.861128

Booth, D. 1998. *The Race Game.* London: Frank Cass.

Booth, D. 2003. Hitting Apartheid for Six? The Politics of the South African Sports Boycott. *Journal of Contemporary History*, 38(3):477–493. https://doi.org/10.1177/0022009403038003008

Cape Times. 4 April 1978.

Cape Times. 5 April 1978.

Cape Times. 22 August 1978.

Cape Town City Football Club Income Statement. 31 October 1977. FASA papers, William Cullen Library, University of the Witwatersrand, South Africa.

Darby, P. 2008. Stanley Rous's 'Own Goal': Football Politics, South Africa and the Contest for the FIFA Presidency in 1974. *Soccer & Society*, 9(2):259–272. https://doi.org/10.1080/14660970701811172

Minutes of SACOS General Meeting. 5 March 1978. F. Cleophas, private collection.

Minutes of SACOS General Meeting. 14 October 1978. F. Cleophas, private collection.

Minutes of SACOS General Meeting. 22 July 1978. F. Cleophas, private collection.

Rand Daily Mail. 19 October 1978.

Rand Daily Mail. 17 November 1978.

SACOS Statement, 6 April 1977. F. Cleophas, private collection.

South African Soccer. February 1978.

South African Soccer. April 1978.

South African Soccer. May 1978.

South African Soccer. August 1978.

South African Soccer. October 1978.

South African Soccer. January 1979.

Venter, G. 2015. Long Balls in the Dying Moments: Exploring the Decline of South Africa's National Football League, 1970–1977. *The International Journal of the History of Sport,* 32(2):265–285. https://doi.org/10.1080/09523367.2014.970635

Venter, G. 2017. Slippery Under Foot: The Shifting Political Dynamics within South African Football, 1973–1976. *South African Historical Journal,* 69(2):265–287. https://doi.org/10.1080/02582473.2016.1257064

From carriers to climbers:
The Cape Province Mountain Club,
1930s to 1960s – an untold story

Farieda Khan
Independent researcher

Introduction

The 87-year-old Cape Province Mountain Club (CPMC) is one of the oldest mountain clubs in South Africa – in fact, only the Mountain Club of South Africa (MCSA) at 127 years of age, is older.[1] However, despite having reached a venerable age, the history of the Club is a largely unknown aspect of South Africa's mountaineering history. One of the reasons for this gap in South African mountaineering history is related to the fact that the MCSA was a club started by and for, the white elite, while the CPMC was established in order to cater for those excluded from it. Thus the story of the CPMC is an integral part of the larger 'hidden history' of the black underclass, a history often hidden from public acknowledgement as a consequence of the subordinate position historically occupied by blacks in South Africa. As a result of the socio-economically and politically subordinate position of blacks, it was inevitable that the history and development of the Club was fundamentally impacted upon and shaped by the political ideology (and the racial hierarchy which underpinned it), of the 1930s–1960s, a period which encompassed the post-Union Segregation era (1910–1947) and the early-to-mid apartheid era (1948–1969). Within the political context of the period under review, this chapter will, by addressing this gap in South African mountaineering history, shed light on the CPMC's untold story.

Historical background to mountaineering at the Cape

The first 'mountaineers' of the Table Mountain Chain (from Signal Hill to Cape Point), were the indigenous Khoi people, whose intimate knowledge of these mountains enabled them to gather roots, nuts and plants for food and traditional medicine, set up their encampments in forest clearings and graze their cattle on the mountain slopes[2] – that is, they interacted with the mountains for survival purposes, not recreation. The roots of mountaineering as a leisure

---

1 Excluding mountain clubs established at schools, such as the South African College School (SACS) Mountain Club, which was established in 1919 (Mountain Club of South Africa c1970s).

2 As noted by the Dutch colonists in the daily journal that they kept from the time the settlement was established in 1652 (Thom 1952:103, 122; Thom 1958:196).

activity in South Africa date back to the era of European exploration which began in the late fifteenth century, when European traders and sailors *en route* to South East Asia stopped at the Cape to take on water and barter for cattle. Here, they took the opportunity for exercise and recreation by walking mountain paths and ascending to the summit of Table Mountain after having been confined to a cramped ship for months on end (Raven-Hart 1967:41, 118).

In the ensuing centuries after colonial settlement in 1652, it was the black underclass, i.e. the servants and slaves, who had an intimate knowledge of the mountains, as a result of their back-breaking daily toil, viz. fetching water, chopping and carrying wood (Van Sittert 2003:163) and doing the laundry in icy mountain streams (Warner & Warner 1985:55). The relationship that the elite had with Table Mountain was mainly in the form of recreation, such as walks, lavish picnics and a "Champagne tiffin" on the summit (Murray 1953:38–39); while visiting scientists and botanists scoured the mountains in search of specimens (Van Sittert 2003:163) – all accompanied by slaves and servants acting as guides and porters (Burchell 1967:34–36; Thunberg 1986:14).

The history of mountaineering as a formal sport may be traced back to the late nineteenth century and the establishment of 'The Mountain Club'[3] in October 1891 (Mountain Club 1894a: 7). The Club, which attracted the cream of the social, professional and governing elite of the Cape (Burman 1966:16), did not specifically bar blacks from membership[4] – however, this was unthinkable, given the growing extent of social segregation based on race in the late colonial era (Bickford-Smith 1995:121–122). Thus, despite the fact that there were many experienced black mountain guides,[5] it seemed that the only role for blacks in the newly-formed MCSA was a subservient one: as cooks, carriers and campsite cleaners.

Given the subordinate status of blacks during the colonial era, the mountain chain was not a recreation space for blacks during this period; however, one remarkable exception was the mountain excursions engaged in by the African students of Zonnebloem College situated in present-day Walmer Estate on the slopes of Table Mountain. From the 1860s onwards, right into the early twentieth century, Zonnebloem students (girls and boys) went on regular mountain walks, accompanied by their teachers, as an integral part of their school programme, as well as during their leisure hours (Hodgson 1975:260–261).

The emergence of the leisure use of the Table Mountain Chain by blacks – early twentieth century

The regular recreational use of the Table Mountain Chain by black (predominantly Coloured) communities may be traced back to the early twentieth century, when the youth in areas with easy access to the mountain, began rambling and hiking on the mountain, as well as engaging in other leisure activities such as swimming in mountain streams, blackberry-picking and collecting pine kernels to make a traditional sweet treat. These areas included Coloured enclaves in central Cape Town (Combrinck 1999; Fredericks 1999; Gool 2000) and in the mainly white suburbs close to the mountain chain, such as Sea Point (Trotter 2002:92), Newlands (Taliep 1992:99, 109); upper Claremont (Taliep 1992:185); Protea Village, below the Kirstenbosch Botanical Garden (Khan 2013); Kalk Bay (Bohlin 2001:278) and Simon's Town

---

3   It was only named the Mountain Club of South Africa in 1910 (Mountain Club of South Africa 1910).
4   There was no reference to race in the Club's Constitution (The Mountain Club 1894b:1).
5   As acknowledged by the MCSA itself (Mountain Club 1892).

(Thomas 2001:96). However, it was in District Six, in which this close connection between the mountain, the natural environment and the community, was particularly evident, as may be seen in the accompanying images. The proximity of the mountain made it easy for the youth of this community to use the mountain environment for recreation, and as an escape from cramped homes and noisy, crowded streets, which were devoid of playparks and green open space (Combrinck 1999, Rassool 2000:3-4). District Six would also prove to be an important nursery of mountaineering talent as a result of the activities of organisations such as the Scouts, the Silvertree Boys' Club, the Marion Institute as well as Anglican missionaries such as the Cowley Brothers (Brian Brock, personal communication, 8 February 2016; Cleophas 2009:188-190; Combrinck 1999; Fredericks 1999; Graham and Walters 2010:78; Kolbe 1999).

The growing popularity of mountain-leisure pursuits such as hiking and camping[6] was such, that by the beginning of the 1930s, the number of Coloured mountain hikers on Table Mountain had increased greatly (Mountain Club of South Africa 1931c). In contrast to the growing trend in mountain-based recreation by the Coloured community, the leisure use of the mountain by African people was extremely limited as a result of the forced removal of Africans from urban areas to racially segregated townships on the outskirts of Cape Town, since the early twentieth century (Goldin 1987:51, 66; Saunders 1984:223). Further, the racial hierarchy in society which arbitrarily placed Africans at the bottom, where they were restricted to the lowest paid, most physically demanding jobs (Goldin 1987:35–36), made it extremely difficult for Africans to participate in mountain-based recreation.

The Cape Province Mountain Club, 1930s–1940s

It was from among the ranks of District-Six-based mountaineers, that the founders and early members of the CPMC were drawn. Early in 1931, the MCSA Treasurer was approached by a "Coloured person" asking for assistance with a view to forming a "Coloured Mountain Club" (Mountain Club of South Africa 1931a). However, it seems that the MCSA offered no assistance and the Cape Province Mountain Club (CPMC) was established in about mid-1931 by a group of enthusiastic mountain climbers in District Six, Cape Town (Mountain Club of South Africa 1931b). Members of the Club were drawn mainly from the lower-middle and working class: for example, the Chairperson, 'Binder' Petersen, was a bookbinder by trade (Cape Province Mountain Club 2012) while others, such as Carl Fisher (Climbing Leader) and Cecil Townshend (Secretary) worked for the City Council as Mountain Rangers (Helen February, personal communication, 25 June 2009; Mountain Club of South Africa 1954b).

The composition of the Club during this period was very likely homogenous, i.e. Coloured and Christian, although in later years the Club has insisted that it was non-racial from the beginning (Odendaal 1993:102). While this claim would be difficult to establish given that the Club's early documents are not available (Peter Bruyns, personal communication, 12 October 2017), it must be noted that this period was one in which sectarianism in sport among black communities was common, with separate organisations based on ethnicity and religion being formed (Grundlingh, Odendaal & Spies 1995:30). Not only was this the case in the Western Cape (District Six Museum 2010:151–153), but some Coloured sports clubs went further, by being overtly hostile to Africans and Muslims, excluding them from membership (Cleophas & Van der Merwe 2011:129; Pick 2015:15-17), competitions and their sports facilities

---

6   George Rudolf, a Scout master, took District Six troops to camp in Table Mountain caves during the 1930s (Combrinck 1999).

(Taliep 2001:69). The CPMC would not have been immune to these trends, hence a likely scenario is that the CPMC was established as a mountaineering organisation for Coloured people, whether this was reflected in its Constitution or not, and that, in all probability, the CPMC remained an organisation for Coloured mountaineers for about the first two decades of its existence.[7] As a former member has acknowledged: "In my parent's time [about the 1940s] it was probably a Coloured club – it's difficult but I think we need to admit it – that's the way things were at that time – of course it changed in later years" (Brian Brock, personal communication, 19 October 2015).

While very little information on the Club's early activities is available, it is however known that the Club carried out mountain rescues with the MCSA, but only informally, as the MCSA was reluctant to establish a formal partnership with the CPMC (Mountain Club of South Africa 1946). The Club was also able to obtain a hut on Table Mountain shortly after its formation in mid-1931 (Mountain Club of South Africa 1931b). Most male members of the Club saw service during WWII, so during this period, the February sisters – Freda, Lily, Joan and Georgina (who all lived in the Bo-Kaap and were the sisters of then Club Chairman, Ronald February) – kept the Club going (Helen February, personal communication, 25 June 2009). The post-war years saw a lot of climbing activity and it was during this period that some of the most talented and self-taught members of the Club came to the fore, many of whom opened new rock climbing routes on Table Mountain. These included Charlie Hankey, Leonard Thomas and Neville Galiet (Brian Brock, personal communication, 19 October 2015).

The relationship between the CPMC and MCSA, 1930s–1940s

Despite claiming to be sympathetic to the establishment of the CPMC, the MCSA preferred to remain aloof, choosing to view the Club merely as a useful mechanism for dealing with the increasing number of black mountaineers (Mountain Club of South Africa 1931c). In fact, the entry of the CPMC into the field of mountaineering represented something of a seismic shock for the MCSA, leaving the Club at a loss as to how to deal with blacks who were fellow mountaineers. While in one sense this was strange, since the two clubs operated mere streets away from each other in central Cape Town, it was also unsurprising since it was a reflection of the unequal power relations that existed between black and white in an era in which racial discrimination and segregation was becoming the norm (Bickford-Smith 1996:14).

The practical consequence of the MCSA's reluctance to engage with the CPMC on a level of equality and collegiality was that the talented climbers in the CPMC were deprived of the opportunity to gain further rock climbing expertise and to learn from their more experienced counterparts in the MCSA.

The Cape Province Mountain Club, 1950s–1960s

The leading climbers during this period included Neville Hendricks, Dick Knipe and Sydney Alexander, who today, is the Club's oldest member (Burman 1966:52; Brian Brock, personal communication, 19 October 2015). Charlie Hankey remained the Club's leading climber, opening new routes on Table Mountain. Unusually for that period, and against the unwritten rules of the MCSA (which frowned on 'mixed' climbing), Hankey had formed a climbing partnership with MCSA member Barry Fletcher (personal communication, 06 October

---

7   Ishmet Allie, who was active in the 1950s, may have been the first Muslim member.

2017). The Club's first expedition abroad was undertaken by three members, to Kilimanjaro in 1951, and the Club's involvement in mountain rescues increased greatly (Cape Province Mountain Club 2011).

The District Six community continued to be a nursery for young mountaineers through the Silvertree Boys' Club under MCSA member David McAdam, and the various scout groups that used the mountain for their activities (Brian Brock, personal communication, 19 October 2015; Gangat 2009; Armien Harris, personal communication, 26 May 2010). Recruitment by the CPMC was mainly through family ties, with the Brock, Abrahams, February, Knipe and Gangat families playing a prominent role in the Club (Darryl Abrahams, personal communication, 07 July 2009; Brian Brock, personal communication, 19 October 2015; Helen February, personal communication, 25 June 2009; Linda Fortune, personal communication, 10 May 2016, Colleen Knipe-Solomon, personal communication, 22 June 2009).

Given the extent of the interest and participation in mountaineering in District Six, it was surprising that the CPMC was not more widely known. However, besides the fact that the Club did not actively recruit outside the circle of family and friends of its members, class and financial factors were also at play, as former member Linda Fortune (personal communication, 10 May 2016) has stated: "[The Club was] very conservative and selective in who they accepted, they were rather elitist. You needed proper boots, a certain amount of equipment – it wasn't cheap – you needed food, a haversack, bus fare, raingear etc."

The beginning of the apartheid era and the institutionalisation of racial discrimination (Thompson 2014:190–191) placed obstacles in the path of black organisations such as the CPMC. For example, the lower salaries earned by blacks (Thompson 2014:195, 200, 202) placed the CPMC at a developmental disadvantage; while the racial prejudice perpetuated by the apartheid system meant that the CPMC could not develop the kind of equal, cordial relationships with white farmers whose land had to be crossed in order to access the mountains in country areas. As a result, the Club sometimes faced hostility from farmers and thus members were restricted in their climbing activities (Colleen Knipe-Solomon, personal communication, 22 June 2009; Patrick Pasqualle, personal communication, 17 August 2017).

While ethnic sectarianism within black sports organisations was largely a spent force by the 1960s (District Six Museum 2010:58, 104), the reality of ethnically segregated residential areas and facilities meant that it would not be until the catalyst of the Soweto Uprising in 1976 that a more radical approach to non-racialism began to be adopted by black sports organisations (Booth 2003:483) and genuine changes to the sporting environment could be made.

The most significant challenge the CPMC faced was the Group Areas Act (Horrell 1978:71), in terms of which District Six was declared a white area in 1966 (Soudien 1990:144). Not only did the subsequent forced removal of the community to the distant Cape Flats end the Club's usual use of venues in the area, it also put paid to the Club's plans to establish a permanent clubhouse in the area (Cape Province Mountain Club 2011). Further, it lost the nursery in which many members of the new generation of mountaineers had been nurtured, and most importantly, it lost the advantage of proximity to Table Mountain. For the District Six community (as indeed for the other communities similarly affected), their eviction from a location so physically close to the mountain was not only traumatic, it also meant a loss of the intimate and positive connection with the mountain that regular and positive interaction had established. Ultimately, the abrupt severance of this physical connection would have negative consequences in the form of an estrangement from the mountain environment of many of the evictees (Combrinck 1999) and even of the next generation.[8]

The relationship between the CPMC and MCSA, 1950s–1960s

The MCSA's acceptance of the apartheid-era ideology of the total separation of the races was a natural evolution from its acceptance of the *de facto* segregation of the first half of the twentieth century. As a result, the relationship between the two clubs continued to be one where the CPMC was mostly ignored[9] and interacted with as infrequently as possible by the MCSA.[10] For the most part, it seemed that the CPMC accepted the nature of its relationship with the MCSA and was resigned to the fact that apartheid ideology dictated this state of affairs. As CPMC member Helen February (personal communication, 25 June 2009) noted of this period: "At that time, we just accepted things as they were – separate clubs – it was the same way in which we accepted all the racial segregation, the boards etc – so we made no overtures [to the MCSA]."

The number of Coloured leisure-seekers on Table Mountain spiked during this period, as observed by the MCSA which regarded this increase as a problem, pointing to the "hordes of undesirable Coloured people" at the Club's annual service, the growing amount of litter on the mountain, as well as crowded, noisy campsites (Mountain Club of South Africa 1955b). As in the past, the MCSA sought to exploit the CPMC as a mechanism to ameliorate these problems, by asking the Club to request its members to keep their campsites clean (Mountain Club of South Africa 1960), despite not having any evidence that it was the CPMC membership that was responsible for littering.

The increase in the number of black mountaineers also led to more 'mixed' climbing partnerships being formed in defiance of the MCSA's unwritten rules, which held that climbing with "Non-Europeans" affected the "prestige" of the Club (Mountain Club of South Africa 1954a), and that invitations to sleep over at the MCSA hut were forbidden (Mountain Club of South Africa 1954a). One member who persisted in defying these conventions was informed that if he continued to choose his "Coloured friends" over his loyalty to the Club, he should resign (Mountain Club of South Africa 1954a). While for the most part, the MCSA's espousal of apartheid was not publicised, by the 1960s the MCSA stated unequivocally in the press: "We only admit whites" and "The Non-whites have their own club, the CPMC" (Mountain Club of South Africa 1962).

By the end of 1960s the CPMC would have been under no illusion about the nature and extent of its relationship with the politically conservative MCSA.

---

8   This alienation is well illustrated by the fact that, in recent years, organisations involved in taking young people from low-income communities on Table Mountain hikes, have found that, in most instances, these excursions are the youngsters' first such experience (Khan 2016).

9   Except for the occasional message of congratulations when the Club reached a significant milestone (Mountain Club of South Africa 1957).

10 Such as a rare invitation to a lecture on rock climbing techniques, which required extraordinary measures to "avoid any embarrassment" – presumably to CPMC members, entering a venue from which apartheid legislation ordinarily excluded them (Mountain Club of South Africa 1955a).

Homepage of the Cape Province Mountain Club
(capeprovince-mountainclub.co.za)

Cape Province Mountain Hut, Table Mountain
(https://www.facebook.com/groups/119458781429347/photos/)

Annual Report of the CPMC, November 2009
(http://capeprovince-mountainclub.co.za/docs/
Mountaineering_Report_Vol3_2009.pdf)

Dirk Ziervogel (front, extreme left) with
'mixed' church group at CPMC Hut, c 1930s
(Personal Collection, Brian Brock)

District Six – at the foot of Table Mountain
(https://za.pinterest.com/pin/663014376362390903/)

Dirk Ziervogel, c 1950s
(Personal Collection, Brian Brock)

The streets were the main playground for the children of District Six
(Photo by Ettiennedup on flickr: https://za.pinterest.com/pin/663014376362390903/)

District Six was declared a white area in 1966
(http://www.districtsix.co.za/Content/Exhibitions/
Interact/Multimedia/LastDays/index.php)

The Founders of the Cape Province Mountain Club,
1931 (http://capeprovince-mountainclub.co.za/index.
php/about)

Conclusion

This chapter has sought to demonstrate that the CPMC was a product of its era: that it was impacted upon and shaped, not only by the racial ideology of the segregation and apartheid eras, but also by the ethnic sectarianism then rampant in black sport. The consequence of these socio-political factors is that co-operation and sharing of expertise across the racial and ethnic divide was not possible, resulting in the development of the sport of mountaineering in general, and among blacks in particular, being stunted.

However, despite the historical stumbling blocks facing the CPMC, the Club was able to harness and build upon the interest in mountaineering that developed among low-income communities living in close proximity to the mountain chain. Despite the indifference, even hostility, displayed by the MCSA at times, the CPMC nonetheless succeeded in creating its own climbing opportunities, as well as helping its members to acquire and develop their rock climbing expertise. In doing so, the CPMC created a positive mountaineering legacy and bequeathed a history which forms an integral part of South African sporting and mountaineering history, one which deserves to be recognised and further explored.

References

Bickford-Smith, V. 1995. *Ethnic Pride and Racial Prejudice in Victorian Cape Town.* Johannesburg: Witwatersrand University Press.

Bickford-Smith, V. 1996. *Representations of Cape Town on the eve of apartheid: Presenting a Social Portrait.* Paper presented at Africa's Urban Past Conference. London.

Bohlin, A. 2001. Places of longing and belonging: Memories of the Group Area Proclamation of a South African fishing village. In Barbara Bender and Margaret Winer (eds.). *Contested landscapes: Movement, exile and place.* Oxford: Berg. 275–287.

Booth, D. 2003. Hitting apartheid for six? The politics of the South African sports boycott. *Journal of South African History*, 38(3):5477–493. https://doi.org/10.1177/0022009403038003008

Burman, J. 1966. *A Peak to Climb.* Cape Town: C. Struik.

Burchell, W.J. 1967. *Travels in the Interior of Southern Africa.* C Struik (Pty) Ltd: Cape Town.

Cape Province Mountain Club. 2011. *A Brief History of the Cape Province Mountain Club.* [Retrieved 13 November 2013] http://capeprovince-mountainclub.co.za/

Cape Province Mountain Club. 2012. *Cape Province Mountain Club.* [Retrieved 13 November 2013] http://capeprovince-mountainclub.co.za/index.php/cpmc

Cleophas, F. 2009. Physical Education and Physical Culture in the Coloured Community of the Western Cape, 1837–1966. PhD thesis. Cape Town: University of Cape Town.

Cleophas, F.J. & Van der Merwe, F.J.G. 2011. Contradictions and Responses concerning the South African Sport Color Bar with special reference to the Western Cape. *African Journal for Physical, Health Education, Recreation and Dance,* 17:124–140.

Combrinck, I. 1999. Transcript of interview by Linda Fortune, 14 September, Table Mountain Interviews, District Six Museum Archives.

District Six Museum. 2010. *Fields of Play: Football Memories and Forced Removals in Cape Town – A District Six Museum Exhibition Catalogue.* Cape Town: District Six and Basler Afrika Bibliographic Publication.

Fredericks, T. 1999. Transcript of interview by Linda Fortune, 14 October, Table Mountain Interviews, District Six Museum Archives.

Gangat, G. 1999. Transcript of interview by Linda Fortune, 05 October, Table Mountain Interviews, District Six Museum Archives.

Gool, M. 2000. Transcript of interview, August, 'Digging Deeper Exhibition', District Six Museum Archives.

Goldin, I. 1987. *Making Race: The Politics and Economics of Coloured Identity in South Africa.* London: Longman.

Graham, S. & Walters, J. (eds). 2010. *Langston Hughes and the South African Drum Generation: The Correspondence.* New York: Palgrave Macmillan. https://doi.org/10.1057/9780230109865

Grundlingh, A., Odendaal, A. & Spies, B. 1995. *Beyond the Tryline – Rugby and South African Society.* Johannesburg: Ravan Press. 143–180.

Hodgson, J.K.H. 1975. A History of Zonnebloem College, 1858 to 1870 – A Study of Church and Society. Master's thesis. Cape Town: University of Cape Town.

Horrell, M. 1978. *Laws affecting Race Relations in South Africa, to the end of 1976.* Johannesburg: South African Institute of Race Relations.

Khan, F. 2013. The Workers of Kirstenbosch – A Tribute. *Veld and Flora*, June:68–70.

Khan, F. 2016. Let's make it second nature. *Saturday Weekend Argus*, 12 June.

Kolbe, V. 1999. Transcript of interview with Vincent by Linda Fortune, 15 September, Table Mountain Interviews, District Six Museum Archives.

Mountain Club, The. 1894a. The Mountain Club, its origin and doings during the first two years. *The Mountain Club Annual*, January 1894:7.

Mountain Club, The. 1894b. Constitution. *The Mountain Club Annual,* January 1894:1–2.

Mountain Club of South Africa. 1892. *The Mountain Club – Sixth Ordinary Monthly Meeting,* 06 April. Special Collections, University of Cape Town, B1.1 Vol. I, 23/10/1891 – 20/11/1895, BC 1421 MCSA.

Mountain Club of South Africa. 1910. *Minutes of a Committee Meeting,* 07 December. Special Collections, University of Cape Town, B1.3 Vol. III, 26/10/1899 – 31/07/1911, BC 1421 MCSA.

Mountain Club of South Africa. 1931a. *A Meeting of the General Committee,* 13 April. Special Collections, University of Cape Town, B1.7 Vol. VII, 13/12/1926 – 11/06/1941, BC 1421 MCSA.

Mountain Club of South Africa. 1931b. *A Meeting of the General Committee,* 13 July 1931. Special Collections, University of Cape Town, B1.7 Vol. VII, 13/12/1926 – 11/06/1941, BC 1421 MCSA.

Mountain Club of South Africa. 1931c. *Annual General Meeting,* 11 December. Special Collections, University of Cape Town, B1.7 Vol. VII, 13/12/1926 – 11/06/1941, BC 1421 MCSA.

Mountain Club of South Africa. 1946. *Annual General Meeting,* 13 December. Special Collections, University of Cape Town, B1.8 Minute Book VIII, 09 June 1941 – 14 December 1949, p. 133. BC 1421 MCSA.

Mountain Club of South Africa. 1954a. *Minutes of a Meeting of the General Committee,* 13 January. *J2.14*, Vol N, 28/01/1939 – 29/12/1956, News Clippings, Special Collections, University of Cape Town, BC 1421 MCSA.

Mountain Club of South Africa. 1954b. *Veteran climber has many memories,* 13 February. B1.9, Vol IX, 09/12/1949 – 09/03/1955, Special Collections, University of Cape Town, BC 1421 MCSA.

Mountain Club of South Africa. 1955a. *Minutes of a Meeting of the General Committee,* 12 January. B1.9, vol IX, 09/12/1949 – 09/03/1955, Special Collections, University of Cape Town, BC 1421 MCSA.

Mountain Club of South Africa. 1955b. *Minutes of a Meeting of the General Committee,* 24 June. B1.9, vol IX, 09/12/1949 – 09/03/1955, Special Collections, University of Cape Town, BC 1421 MCSA.

Mountain Club of South Africa. 1957. *Minutes of a Meeting of the General Committee,* 09 January. B1.10, vol X, 25/03/1955 – 18/12/1961, Special Collections, University of Cape Town, BC 1421 MCSA.

Mountain Club of South Africa. 1960. *Minutes of a Meeting of the General Committee,* 08 June. B1.10, vol X, 25/03/1955 – 18/12/1961, Special Collections, University of Cape Town, BC 1421 MCSA.

Mountain Club of South Africa. 1962. "Quit racists ex-judge told". News Clippings, 07 September. J2.16, vol P, 1961–1965, Special Collections, University of Cape Town, BC 1421 MCSA.

Mountain Club of South Africa. c1970s. "Climbing". News Clippings. J2.24, 1969 – 1977, Special Collections, University of Cape Town, BC 1421 MCSA.

Murray, J. (ed). 1953. *In Mid-Victorian Cape Town – Letters from Miss Rutherfoord.* Cape Town: A.A. Balkema.

Odendaal, L. 1993. Climbing to Greater Heights, Together. *Tribute,* November:100–102.

Pick, W. 2015. *One for the Chuck – Glimpses into the History of the Maitland-Parow and Districts Cricket Union, 1912–1976.* Cape Town: Western Province Cricket Association and Cricket South Africa.

Rassool, Y. 2000. *District Six – Lest we forget.* Cape Town: University of the Western Cape.

Raven-Hart, R. 1967. *Before van Riebeeck – Callers at South Africa from 1488-1652.* Cape Town: C. Struik (Pty) Ltd.

Saunders, C. 1984. The Creation of Ndabeni – Urban Segregation and African Resistance in Cape Town. In: Christopher Saunders (ed.). *Studies in the History of Cape Town.* Cape Town: Centre for African Studies, University of Cape Town. 165–193.

Soudien, C. 1990. District Six: From Protest to Protest. In: Shamil Jeppie and Crain Soudien (eds). *The Struggle for District Six – Past and Present.* Cape Town: Buchu Books. 143-180.

Taliep, W. 2001. Belletjiesbos, Draper Street and the Vlak – Coloured Neighborhoods of Claremont before the Group Areas Act. *African Studies,* 60(1):65–85. https://doi.org/10.1080/00020180120063683

Thom, H.B. (ed). 1952. *Journal of Jan van Riebeeck, 1652-1655,* vol. I. Cape Town: A.A. Balkema.

Thom, H.B. (ed). 1958. *Journal of Jan van Riebeeck, 1659-1662,* vol. III. Cape Town: A.A. Balkema.

Thomas, A. 2001. It changed everybody's lives: The Simon's Town Group Areas Removals. In: Sean Field (ed.). *Lost Communities, Living Memories – Remembering Forced Removals in Cape Town.* Cape Town: David Philip. 81–97.

Thompson, L. 2014. *A History of South Africa – From the earliest known human habitation to the present*. South Africa: Jonathan Ball Publishers.

Thunberg, C.P. 1986. *Travels at the Cape of Good Hope, 1772–1775*. V.S. Forbes (ed.). Cape Town: Van Riebeeck Society.

Van Sittert, L. 2003. The bourgeois eye aloft: Table Mountain in the Anglo urban middle class imagination, c.1891–1952. *Kronos – Journal of Cape History,* 29:161–190.

Warner, B. & Warner, N. (eds.). 1985. *Journal of Lady Jane Franklin at the Cape of Good Hope, November 1836*. Cape Town: Friends of the South African Library.

[faded newspaper masthead text]

100 YARDS HANDICAP.
Boys under 10.

Willie Mackinon ... .
Michael Miller ... .
Pieter Retief.. .. ..
Edward Miller.. .. ..
Won by 2 yards; 1 yard between second and third.

120 YARDS HANDICAP.
Boys under 14.

Pieter Retief, 10 years .. ..
Michael Mackinon, 13 years .. .. ..
Willie Kenman, 12 years .. ..
Hen Jacobs, 14 years .. ..
Willie Rennie, 12 years .. ..
Michael Miller, 12 years .. ..
Isaac Abrams, 11 years .. ..

"The sound of the hickory": Baseball, colonisation and decolonisation

Hendrik Snyders

Head of Department, History, National Museum Bloemfontein and
Research Associate, History Department, Stellenbosch University

Introduction

Foreign sporting codes such as baseball, Australian football, hurling, Cornish wrestling and lacrosse arrived in South Africa on the back of the influx of foreigners in the wake of the discovery of diamonds in Griqualand West and gold on the Witwatersrand from the mid- to late 19th century. During the course of the century, large numbers of immigrants established themselves in Cape Town, Johannesburg, Pretoria and Durban where they set up various sport clubs. These clubs offered leisure pastimes of 'home', served as meeting places for new arrivals and facilitated their integration into the new social environment (Gillett 1988:174). It also assisted in combating boredom as well as providing the "spirit with elasticity" in the desolate mining towns (Gutsche 1966:42). The institutions that catered for British sports, over time became more than recreation facilities "for athletic pursuits and for the various branches of bodily games" (Gutsche 1966:14) but served as spaces of social status and political domination in which "the imperialists celebrated their Britishness, authority and imperial lifestyle" (Odendaal 1988:190). As such they are an an integral part of the colonisation project.

Baseball, America's favourite sport, made a relatively late entry into South Africa despite the existence of significant pockets of American citizens all over the country. Little evidence also exists to indicate that either the members of the Church of Christ of Latter Day Saints, which has been an operational presence since 1853 (Monson 1971), or the sizeable African-American population in Cape Town promoted or played the game locally (Charles 2004). According to contemporary newspaper evidence, the first organised baseball games were played on the Witwatersrand between 1893 and 1895. Rosenthal (1968:171) traced the first recorded game back to a match between American gold diggers and mine engineers on the grounds of the Wanderers Club in 1893. Gutsche (1966:42), however, claimed that the first such match actually took place on Sunday, 10 February 1895 at the Old Wanderers Club between the mining teams of Simmer & Primrose versus City and Robinson. This notwithstanding, the inauguration of the "exciting and at the same time perfectly safe game" (*Wagga Wagga Advertiser* 1889:2; *Mount Barker Courier* 1889:2) in South Africa came two decades after its introduction to the United Kingdom (*Sydney Mail & New South Wales Advertiser* 1874:394) and a decade after the game was introduced to Australia.

In accordance with the established social practices, participation in the early games in South Africa was restricted to white players-only since, as the *Cape Argus* suggested, "the races are best socially apart, each good in their own way, but a terribly bad mixture" (Bickford-Smith 1995:149). Baseball therefore became an integral part of the marginalisation of blacks and the colonisation process from the onset. Unsurprisingly, this aspect is either ignored or underplayed in the existing scholarship (Chetwynd 2008; Grundlingh 2017). Concomitantly, with the exception of the work of Cleophas and Van der Merwe (2011), the contribution of black baseballers in the shaping, further development and liberation of the game from segregation and apartheid are completely ignored. This state of affairs, noted Clevenger (2017:1) in a different context, "stymie the possibility of giving historical and poetic representation to non-Western and pre-modern modes of knowledge". Ironically, there is a growing body of literature on the decolonisation of baseball in other parts of the world (Taiwan, Japan, etc.) which has stripped the game of its innocence. This chapter aims to contribute to this process and firstly starts by providing some historical detail about the evolution of the South African game from the late 19th century up to 1960. Secondly, it aims to foreground the role of baseball in the colonisation process and to make a case for a process of decolonisation that Appadurai (2015:1) suggested is essentially "a dialogue with the colonial past, and not a simple dismantling of colonial habits and modes of life".

Transvaal pioneers: rooting a colonial game

The Transvaal Americans, noted Chetwynd (2008:73), "were true missionaries for the sport, bringing equipment, creating a baseball diamond, and setting up games". Playing initially on an informal base on Simmer & Jack and City & Suburban mines properties, out of these activities emerged two of South Africa's first baseball clubs, the Johannesburg Baseball Club and the May Stars Baseball Club. By the turn of the century, with 37 active players in Johannesburg, an official league could be set up. The Anglo-Boer/South African War, however, interrupted its potential expansion and consolidation. Since most of the playing members joined the war effort on either side of the conflict, baseball was further drawn into the process of colonising South Africa.

During the war period a number of informal matches such as between the 'Majors', 'Colonels' and between quasi-national teams such as 'Canada', and 'America' were played at the Wanderers. The latter event netted a gate of £50 that was donated to the Nazareth Home in the city. These activities were not restricted to baseball. Similar matches were occasionally played in football, rugby ("Colonial-born versus Home Born") and lacrosse during the course of the century as a means to promote their game and to express their distinctive [foreign] identities, emphasise their 'otherness' and distinguish them from the indigenous population (Snyders 2016:99).

At the end of the war, the process of rebuilding the game started in earnest and over the course of the first decade of the new century, at least seven clubs were established. This laid the foundation for the formation of the all-white Transvaal Baseball Association (TBA) in September 1904. Its affiliated members included Johannesburg, South African Constabulary, Pretoria, 'Internationals', Old Edwardians, Wanderers, Old Maristonians and Crescents baseball clubs. This created considerable optimism and hope for the future amongst its promotors who provided reports to both their American and Australian media.

From the outset, the game's administrators and interested others published players' game statistics, their qualities and reported on the nature of their facilities. These were carried in newspapers such as the *Washington Post* and a variety of local and regional papers in Australia. The deliberate creation of records and archives were undoubtedly aimed at modelling the Transvaal Baseball Association on a wider system, to demonstrate their knowledge of the rules of the game and to portray itself as a competent and legitimate institution (Snyders 2016:106–7). A sport record:

> is a widely acknowledged statistically stated, supreme athletic performance of a recognised kind. The record is abstract in that it exists apart from the performance itself and recognizes only what is remarkable about the performance. The record exists apart from chronological time, geography and any social distinction or distinctions of the person or persons who establish it (Mandell 1975:4).

The meticulous recording of player statistics and constructing a record of their relative abilities within this context and the need to have it 'publicly' certify as recognised performances within a segregated context, are acts of colonisation. It also helped to further cement the established epistemic standard for a history based on documents and familiar with the "compositional logics of archival imaginaries" (El Shakry 2015:920).

Contemporary reports indicated that American sailors who visited Cape Town and Durban, played baseball amongst themselves during their spare time and on shore leave. Due to the irregularity of these visits and the absence of a dedicated following, the game, seemingly, struggled to establish a foothold. Although a group of black Americans established the American Sporting Club in Cape Town in 1908, the available evidence gave no indication of whether they played any baseball publicly. During their three decades of existence, they, however, participated in the annual Coon Carnival and routinely used American symbolism to distinguish themselves (Charles 2004:51). The game was also invisible in other parts of the country in the period before the outbreak of the First World War in 1914. During the ensuing period, the game's progress was severely disrupted and under difficult wartime conditions, nearly died.

Post-war development – religion, race and politics, 1928–1956

After a decade of paralysis caused by the immediate post-war conditions, the Transvaal Baseball Association (TBA) was reconstituted on 27 April 1928 under the leadership of R.W. Rusterholz (President). This started a process of reorganisation both in terms of competition and the regularisation of membership following earlier attempts by established clubs to deny others membership for fear of losing their playing members (Donaldson 1949). The restart of the Transvaal operation had beneficial effects and stimulated the formation of other provincial associations such as Natal (1931), Western Province (1932) and Eastern Province (1934), each with their own inter-club leagues (Brink 1943:9). The existence of a number of provincial units also gave rise to the institution of the playing of inter-provincial games and the establishment of the South African Baseball Board (SABB) in December 1934.

In accordance with the established social practices, these organisations remained all white. In the case of the Western Province, the provincial body was established with the active involvement of American missionaries associated with the Church of Jesus Christ of Latter Day Saints. One of the central beliefs of "Mormon policymaking and interpretation" closely associated with its founding fathers Joseph Smith and Brigham Young was the view "that blacks were the cursed posterity of the Cain/Ham/Canaan lineage". As a result, and for a significant period of time, their missionaries in South Africa were not interested in the Christian conversion of the South African indigenous population but rather in increasing membership amongst members of the white population (Alston 2014:111–2). Thus, as the missionary group under the leadership Don Mack Walton (Head of the Mission of the Church) embarked on the popularisation of their religion with the aid of baseball (*Deseret News* 15 July 1935), they became complicit in the colonising process. Clubs such as Cumorah, Nomads, and the Wembley Americans, had a direct link to the church and had no problem with playing in the all-white competition. This orientation accompanied the Johannesburg Baseball Club on their tour of Australia in 1935 where they actively promoted the idea of reciprocal tours by national teams (*Sydney Morning Herald* 1935). Since tours served the purpose of both displaying progress and telling "stories about themselves to their fellow citizens and global audiences" (Dyreson 1995:23), the touring team became an ideological representative and flag-carrier of segregation.

By the start of the Second World War, 150 clubs were actively playing the game in organised competitions nationally. This was aided by the fact that several multi-code sports clubs from 1934 onwards added baseball to their club programmes (*Schenectady Gazette* 1934). By the time that the USS Boise arrived in Cape Town at the end of 1938, the game was thriving. This growth received a further boost when the Americans played three games including against a combined all-white South African team that was won by the visitors. In Western Province, in particular, the number of clubs increased from seven in 1932 to 33 in less than a decade. In this process, Paarl and Stellenbosch became important rural nodes for the game beyond Cape Town. This exposed a larger section of the [black] urban and peri-urban community to the sport. The outbreak and duration of the war, however, significantly disrupted this strong spurt of growth.

In the immediate aftermath of the war, the growth in the number of active clubs was initially slow. Interest in the game, however, remained strong. Following a period of steady growth in the ranks of white fans, there were 73 clubs nationally at the end of the 1949 season. This growth followed an initial attempt by the national body to initiate international tours to, amongst others, Australia. On the fringes of these events, media reports about the existence of a parallel [black] baseball tradition in various Coloured neighbourhoods in Cape Town started to emerge. In addition to reports about activity in the Maitland area, the city-southern suburb axis emerged as a particular stronghold with clubs existing in Newlands (St Andrews Dodgers), District Six (City Wolves and Olympic Swifts), Crawford (Ohio Cubs) and Mowbray (Mowbraves) (Cleophas & Van der Merwe 2011:226). The act of naming, noted Nauright (1998:62), extends beyond mere social and "cultural mimicking" but formed part of a complex and "elaborate process of proving respectability" and the pursuit of social advancement. These name choices were seemingly an attempt to link the sport's cultural heartland, history and traditions with the local community's present and past struggles. These clubs also formed the nucleus of the Western Province Baseball Union (WPBU), established in May 1950. A year later, the Western Province Softball Union for women was formed. The two bodies amalgamated three years later to form one umbrella controlling structure catering for both sexes. This coincided with the rollout of a government programme of institutionalised racism (apartheid) which had further implications for the further development of the game and its part in the colonisation project.

Following its electoral victory in 1948, the National Party of D.F. Malan promulgated various laws to institutionalise the segregation of the races. Under this dispensation, sport officially became a segregated affair with the best sports facilities and the right to represent South Africa internationally, reserved for white athletes. Lacking its own facilities, the black WPBU was forced to use municipal facilities, including a piece of land, belonging to the City of Cape Town in the suburb of Athlone. In addition, the Maitland Sports Ground became the alternate venue for the hosting of games. The formal introduction of organised games in the central part of Cape Town encouraged others to follow suit. In 1951, a number of clubs located in the southern suburbs and South Peninsula area established the Cape District Baseball and Softball Union (CDBSU) with the Princeton Sports Ground in Wynberg as its headquarters. These developments coincided with the launch of the first official inter-provincial tournament under the auspices of the white SA Baseball Board (SABB). The 1951/2 season also witnessed the further immersion of baseball into the cauldron of the country's racial politics.

In addition to the rollout of their racial programme, the fourth year of National Party rule saw the culmination of two years of planning to celebrate the arrival of European colonialisation of South Africa by the Dutch East India Company in 1652. At the outset of the planning in 1950, the organisers of the Van Riebeeck Festival decided to include sports into the programme to symbolise specifically the role of amateur sport in the building of a nation. Furthermore, the delegates from the various white sporting federations decided that the festival should be one in which "both European language groups would feel at home either as participants or sightseers" (Western Cape Archives and Records Services). The black sporting tradition clearly was of no significance. The Festival's sub-committee on the participation of Coloureds, Malays and Griquas, however, resolved to include a float in the main festival procession to represent sport in these communities. Given the obvious ideological objectives underpinning the festival, especially its explicit aim of celebrating European civilisation and colonisation, anti-apartheid groups including the African National Congress issued a call for blacks to boycott the event. These circumstances undoubtedly contributed to a reluctance on the part of the American government to officially take part in the festivities.

As part of their contribution to the festivities, the white baseball and softball fraternity proposed to host an inter-provincial tournament in Cape Town and to conclude their tournament with the playing of a South African team against the Rest (Western Cape Archives and Records Services). The former plan was confirmed in January 1952 with Rosebank earmarked as the main venue. The Church of Jesus Christ of Latter Day Saints accepted the role of official ticket seller for the scheduled tournament (Cape Archives Repository 1952). To stimulate further interest in their programme, the baseball organisers announced plans to bring an overseas team to the festival scheduled for 9-16 February 1952. This ambitious plan, however, failed and the festival matches were converted into the inaugural interprovincial tournament inclusive of South West Africa (present-day Namibia) and Rhodesia (present-day Zimbabwe). This event coincided with the coaching tour and favourable public statements about the state of white baseball talent of American baseball coach, John Burrows (*Eikestad Nuus* 1952).

The pride and confidence of white South Africa was soon challenged. The African National Congress (ANC), supported by a significant number of liberal whites, embarked on a civil disobedience campaign, the "Defiance of Unjust Laws Campaign" in 1952 to signal their rejection of apartheid. Represented in a range of organisations including the Black Sash, Liberal Party, South African Communist Party and Progressive Party, were notable figures such as Joe Slovo, Albie Sachs, Helen Suzman and a range of others (Suzman 1993). The apartheid government responded with vehemence and unleashed a campaign of intimidation and bullying against its opposition. It also enacted further legislation to counter the burgeoning domestic anti-apartheid movement.

Rejuvenated by its first inter-provincial tournament, the successful Burrows-coaching programme and growth that extended into South West Africa and Rhodesia, the SA Baseball Board brimmed with confidence as it entered the second half of the decade. This confidence was further strengthened by the arrival of the USS *Midway* in Cape Town in January 1955. On a world tour, the ship's scheduled docking in Cape Town soon became controversial as concerns arose about the applicability of the apartheid laws to the *Midway*'s black crew members while in South African waters. Given the ship's significant number of non-white crew (400), the American Consul-General deemed it appropriate to pre-warn the US Naval authorities about the applicability of South Africa's apartheid laws to these members while on shore leave. The possibility of having to segregate these sailors from their white counterparts during their two-day stay immediately raised concern and protest to the Navy Secretary and the Secretary of State by two Senators and the National Association for the Advancement of Coloured Peoples (NAACP). They also demanded that docking in Cape Town be cancelled since it was standard naval protocol to observe local law and custom when in port and that visiting the city would make the Navy guilty of collaborating with apartheid. This request was, however, ignored since the visit, in the words of the naval authorities, was prompted by an "operational logistical requirement" (*Cape Argus* 1955).

Prior to their docking on 15 January, the crew was briefed on all South African laws. The black crew, in particular, was informed that while on shore, all apartheid laws would be applicable and that liquor, for example, could only be procured from establishments reserved for non-whites. Otherwise, everybody was invited to an [all-white] baseball game between the 'Midway Comets' [the ship's official team] and a local team at Hartleyvale. Furthermore, the US Consul-General, together with the ship's commanding officer and the Department of Coloured Affairs, further arranged a match between the *Midway*'s black officers and the team of the Cape District Baseball Union. Through these acts, baseball yet again became complicit in promoting segregation and apartheid. Far from being an isolated incident, the same situation was repeated during the latter part of the season with the arrival of a USA Amateur baseball team for a 33-match tour. Mindful of the events during the *Midway* visit, the SA Baseball Board issued the visitors with a letter, offering advice on 'table manners and the social amenities', including handling of race issues and the 'colour question', political protocols, handling and approaching women and the subtleties of language (*Milwaukee Journal* 1956:40). The visitors did not only complete their tour but seemingly also had no problem with being restricted to playing whites-only opposition.

The continued exclusion of black athletes from competing on an equal footing with their white counterparts created significant resentment and demands for equality in all areas of life. Black demands for sport equality voiced by the Coordinating Committee for International Recognition (CCIR – est. 1955) led by Port Elizabeth activist Dennis Brutus, were, however, ignored. Realising the need for unified action, black baseballers in the Western Province,

Eastern Province and Griqualand West gathered in Port Elizabeth in September 1956 and established the South African Baseball and Softball Federation (SABSF) to coordinate its affairs. Two years later, this body became one of the eight founding members of the South African Sports Association (SASA) following the demise of the CCIR because of state repression (Smit 2010:10). Despite significant support amongst affiliates based within the oppressed communities, SASA's attempts to negotiate fundamental change from within failed dismally. This forced the organisation's leadership to lobby international federations directly in the hope of forcing a change of the status quo. In addition, SASA attempted to persuade corporate sponsors to make rejection of racism a precondition for their support of white sport events (Brutus 1962). This was met by further state repression and the denial of travel document to black anti-apartheid sport administrators as the decade ended. As South Africa entered the 1960s, baseball was fully part of the apartheid project.

Conclusion

South African baseball is as complicit and tainted by its involvement in colonisation as its counterparts elsewhere in the world. As the historical record indicates, it was not only comfortable with the existing exclusionary practices, but it actively participated in ensuring that the status quo remained and that white culture and practices remained a distinctive instrument of identification and 'otherness' in a foreign world. True to the basic tenets of Western epistemology, it also pioneered the creation of official records and archives to ensure that 'history without archives' and unrecorded performances would enjoy no recognition. Through this, it ensured that the alternative voice and concomitant sporting legacy and tradition were silenced and the human beings behind the voices reduced to invisibility. Establishment baseball, through its further expropriation of tours, international coaching clinics and quasi-international contests, further denied black players an opportunity to tell their stories to the world and to display their undoubted prowess to global audiences in their own particular way. Its general comfortability and active participation in the creation of racially separate competitions, honours and spaces and its enthusiastic celebration of colonial domination as demonstrated by the Van Riebeeck Festival, forcefully emphasised why South African baseball history is in dire need of decolonisation.

References

Alston, B.T. 2014. Transatlantic Latter-day Saints: Mormon Circulations between America and South Africa. PhD Dissertation (Religious Studies), University of Cape Town (February).

Appadurai, A. 2015. Playing with modernity: The decolonisation of Indian Cricket. *Altre Moderna* 14:1–25.

Athletes visiting Africa make friends for America. *The Milwaukee Journal*, February 1956.

"Baseball is king", *Schenectady Gazette*, 24 April 1934.

Bickford-Smith, V. 1998. Leisure and social identity in Cape Town, British Cape Colony, 1938–1988. *Kronos: Journal of Cape History*, 25(1):103–128.

"Bofbal afrigter na Stellenbosch." *Eikestad Nuus*, 1 Maart 1952.

Brenner, F.H. 1914. Baseball. In *The Transvaal Leader*, 1914, *South African Sport*; Johannesburg.

Brink, J.A. 1943. Ontwikkeling van Bofbal in die Westelike Provinsie. B.Ed. (Phil) Dissertation. Stellenbosch University (November).

Charles, M.J. 2004. "Soort soek soort": The "American Negro" Community in Cape Town Until 1930. M.A. (Historical Studies) Dissertation, University of Cape Town.

Chetwynd, J. 2008. A history of South African baseball. *Nine: A Journal of Baseball History and Culture*, 16(2), (Spring):73–79.

Clevenger, S.M. 2017. Sport history, modernity and the logic of coloniality: a case for decoloniality. *Rethinking History: The Journal of Theory and Practice*, 21(4):586–605.

The Deseret News, 15 July 1935. https://doi.org/10.1080/13642529.2017.1326696

Donaldson, A. *The South African Sporting Encyclopaedia and Who's Who.* Johannesburg: Donaldson Publications, 1949.

Dyreson, M. 1995. Marketing National Identity: The Olympic Games of 1932 and American Culture. *Olympika: The International Journal of Olympic Studies IV*:23–48.

El Shakry, O. 2015. "History without documents": The vexed archives of decolonization in the Middle East. *American Historical Review,* 120(3):920–934. https://doi.org/10.1093/ahr/120.3.920

Gillett, R. 1988. Where the big men fly: An early history of Australian Football in the Riverina, *Sporting Traditions*, 4(2).

Grundlingh, M. 2017. South Africa: The battle for baseball. In G. Gmelch & D.A. Nathan (eds.). *Baseball Beyond our Borders: An International Pastime*. Lincoln & London: University of Nebraska Press. https://doi.org/10.2307/j.ctt1kgqvd6.23

Gutsche, T. 1966. *Old Gold: The History of the Wanderers Club*, Cape Town: Howard Timmins.

Mandell, R.D. 1975. The idea of a sports record. *LA84 Foundation: NASSH Proceedings*. Available from: library.la84.org/SportsLibrary/NASSH_Proceedings/NP1975/NP1975c. pdf. [Accessed 22 August 2017].

"Midway Captain is satisfied with plans for Negro sailors." *Cape Argus*, 15 January 1955.

Monson, F.R. 1971. History of the South African Mission of the Church of Jesus Christ of Latter Day Saints 1853–1970. M.A. Dissertation (Church History & Doctrine), Brigham Young University (May).

Nauright, J. 1998. *Sport, Cultures, and Identities in South Africa.* Claremont: David Phillip.

Odendaal, A. 1988. South Africa's Black Victorians: Sport and society in South Africa in the Nineteenth Century. In J.A. Mangan (ed.). *Pleasure, profit, proselytism: British culture and sport at Home and Abroad: 1700 –1914*. London: Frank Cass & Co.

Rosenthal, E. 1968. *Stars and Stripes in Africa*, Cape Town: National Books Limited.

Smit, J.A. 2010. Dennis Brutus: Activist for Non-racialism and Freedom of the Human Spirit. *Alternation* 17(2):8–71.

Snyders, H. 2016. 'Old friends at the game in Africa': The origins and early development of lacrosse in Natal, South Africa. *Sporting Traditions*, 33(2):93–109.

"South African invitation", *Sydney Morning Herald*, 1 July 1935.

Suzman, H. 1993. *In No Uncertain Terms: Memoirs.* Johannesburg: Jonathan Ball.

"Telegraphic Intelligence". *The Wagga Wagga Advertiser* (NSW), 16 March 1889.

University of the Witwatersrand Historical Papers Archive, South African Institute of Race Relations Collection, AD 1715: D.A. Brutus (South African Sports Association – Appeal to All Olympic Councils, 1 January 1962 and D.A. Brutus (South African Sports Association) – The Manager: Hullett's Sugar Refinery, 16 July 1962.

"Via San Francisco – Great Britain", *The Sydney Mail and New South Wales Advertiser*, 26 September 1874.

Western Cape Archives Services, KAB, Accessions 709: Van Riebeeck Tercentenary Festival: Volume 5: Minutes of the Sports Sub Committee: 24 November 1950 – 17 January 1952.

ACCOUNTS FROM THE COALFACE

One for the Chuck: Glimpses into the history of the Maitland-Parow and Districts Cricket Union

William Pick

Professor Emeritus and former Head of the School of Public Health, Witwatersrand University
Honorary Professor, University of Cape Town
Extra-ordinary Professor, Stellenbosch University

An examination of the history of the Maitland-Parow and Districts Cricket Union reveals an incredible process of transformation from a British colonial gentleman's game to a rallying point of progressive forces in a society striving for political rights and social equity. It is this historical process, which mimics the experience of so many colonised populations all over the world, that makes itself known through the fascinating sixty-five-year journey of the Maitland-Parow and Districts Cricket Union.

I felt that I needed to contribute, albeit in a small way, to the struggle to produce a decolonised South African history that more fully represents the experience of those who have traditionally been excluded from official accounts and whose histories had been distorted through the process of falsification. I will spend a bit of time telling you about cricket life in the northern areas of Cape Town. Professor André Odendaal was part of creating this book, *One for the Chuck*, unlocked financial support for me and had a lot to do with layout and production of the book.[1] Others who should be thanked include the Western Province Cricket Association and Cricket South Africa who provided financial support, John Young, who proofread many versions of the manuscript and suggested the mapping of the playing fields to demonstrate the effects of the Group Areas Act,[2] the interviewees who so willingly contributed by telling their stories, as well as those who provided minutes of meetings, photographs, press reports and scorebooks.

The primary purpose of the work was to memorialise the activities of players and administrators who participated in the game of cricket in the northern suburbs of Cape Town from 1912 to 1976. We usually write about the stars, the high achievers, the champions.

---

1   The Western Province Cricket Association set up a History Committee in 1998 in response to the United Cricket Board of South Africa's Transformation Charter (Allie M. 2000 *More than a game*, p. 8). *One for the Chuck* is part of this initiative.
2   The Group Areas Act of 1950 assigned racial groups to separate residential and business sections in urban areas. An effect of this Act was that it prevented non-whites from living in the most developed areas.

And that is quite appropriate. There is nothing wrong with that. What the book tries to do, however, is revisionist in nature by highlighting the participation of players from the lower divisions and more junior teams in the Maitland-Parow and Districts Cricket Union (MPDCU),[3] in addition to those who represented the union at national, provincial and senior levels. From about 1970 a challenge was directed to the prevailing liberal view of South Africa's historical scholars' materialist view of the past. Revisionists concerned themselves with the nature of South Africa's political structures in terms of its economic development.

The book further reflects on the interaction between cricket and socio-political events of the time. It also demonstrates the role of sport, in general, and cricket in particular, in rallying ordinary people and their communities around deeply moral issues – issues of fair play, equality, and respect for one's fellow human being, including one's opponents.[4] The history of the MPDCU provides evidence of a vibrant community organisation. At a local and community level, cricket was an extraordinary vehicle for social coherence, democracy and self-reliance. There was effectively no funding from sources in those days. People raised their own funds, they created the sport, prepared the playing fields themselves, players carried and laid the mats themselves, on pitches that they had to prepare themselves. The activities of cricket clubs were, to a large extent, based on self-generated enthusiasm. It was wonderful to see from the reading and from the work we did how involved communities were.

The MPCDU was established in 1912, at a time when there was an attempt to strengthen cricket in the Western Cape by amalgamation of unions. The union was part of a struggling provincial cricket organisation that said unions should combine to form one big organisation. By 1932 the Maitland-Parow Districts Cricket Union was one of four unions that participated in the Peninsula and Western District Cricket Board. The other unions were the Metropolitan and Suburban, Somerset West and Paarl-Wellington Unions (Pick 2015:57).

As the name indicated, clubs were predominantly from the area between Maitland and Parow, but the districts affiliated to the union were spread to include Kuilsriver,[5] Bellville,[6] Kraaifontein,[7] Elsies River[8] and as far away as Malmesbury.[9] Some teams had their playing

---

[3]   The suburb, Maitland, is located in the northern parts of Cape Town. It grew out of a slum-clearing project at the turn of the 20th century and was incorporated into the Cape Town municipality in 1913. After the Second World War the government built 60 flats for white ex-servicemen. In August 1954, plans were advertised for official segregation in Maitland (Bickford-Smith V., et. al 1999. *Cape Town in the twentieth century*, pp. 19, 46,123, 169).

[4]   These issues were also visible in the Makana Football Association, formed by the political prisoners on Robben Island in June 1969, Korr C & Close M. 2008. *More than just a game*, pp. 72, 75.

[5]   A semi-urban area 18 kilometres outside Cape Town.

[6]   During the 1960s, the northern parts of Bellville, some 24 kilometres outside Cape Town, represented the contemporary strength of Afrikaner capitalism, Bickford-Smith V., et al. 1999. *Cape Town in the twentieth century*, p. 186. Bellville South was segregated for people of colour.

[7]   A semi-urban area about 27 kilometres outside of Cape Town.

[8]   By 1940 there were an estimated 50,000 coloured people living in the Elsies River area, and in 1942 it was labelled as one of the "black spots" in the Cape Peninsula due to an ever-increasing population, sanitation and other health issues, and high infant mortality rates (2 out if every 10 babies die before age one), Elsie's River, Wikipedia. From the 1960s till the present Elsies River is a non-white, largely sub-economic area, Weeder M. 2006. *The palaces of memory*, pp. 91–92; Bickford-Smith V., et al. 1999. *Cape Town in the twentieth century*, p. 88.

[9]   A semi-rural town, some 70 kilometres outside Cape Town.

fields on the Green Point Common and later, Bishop Lavis Township[10] and Mannenberg.[11] The period covers the early days of the Union of South Africa, through the dark days of apartheid, and reflects the legacy of colonialism through its effects on cricket, as well as the compounded inequity of apartheid sport. The book was particularly focused on providing information about cricket at union level, as this was the real cauldron of contest, given that provincial tournaments took place only once every four years.

The first thing I need to share with readers is that records of local other-than-white cricket units are very scanty. In South Africa the media colluded with the apartheid regime when they printed race-based 'extra' or 'special' editions for cricket organisations of colour. When I tried to recover these records at the National Library, I was told that they do not exist. It seems that the apartheid-colluding media had successfully covered their tracks.

Another feature of the work was that it provided a glimpse of cricket internationalism. Cricket, as an agent of British imperialism, manifested itself through the annexation of foreign lands and the imposition of British laws and culture. Such manifestation was reflected in the relationship between industrial magnates and cricket, after whom trophies were named (Allen 2008:443–471).

The impact of the great depression in the 1930s on cricket in the Maitland-Parow and Districts Cricket union was another example of cricket's reflection of the international experience. The global economic collapse manifested itself at local level through a decline in individual club membership and club distintegration. Unemployment led to many clubs struggling to raise subscriptions from members and the number of clubs and teams declined. Efforts were made to cut costs. Old, used cricket balls were recycled, cricket tours were cancelled and the annual presentation dance was cancelled owing to lack of support. Trophies were thus presented to successful players at the final Annual Meeting, a practice which continued for a number of seasons. The situation became so bad that the MPDCU could only afford to provide tea to visiting teams and stopped providing refreshments to its own players at Board matches.

Another consequence of the Great Depression was that tours were cancelled and players who had been selected could not compete at higher level (Pick, 2015:12–15).

Players who represented the union had to pay the cost of participating in the matches themselves. It became difficult for players who played inter-provincial tournaments (which happened every four years) to pay their own travel costs and the union was obliged to pay. However, in 1937 the union could only afford to pay for third-class train tickets to get the players to the Port Elizabeth tournament. In order to support clubs the union sold second-hand cricket balls to clubs at eight shillings each. Clubs were granted two months to pay for the ball.

The extreme cost-saving practices also had some interesting consequences. One of the most amusing events occurred when Avenirs (established 1910) and Magnolia B (established

---

10 A sub-economic area located 15 kilometres east of Cape Town. In 2001 it had a population of 44,419 people, of whom 97% described themselves as Coloured, and 90% spoke Afrikaans while 9% spoke English.

11 The township of Mannenberg was created for some displaced people of District Six. In 1972, Raymond Hill, writing in the *Cape Herald*, said: "Mannenberg – the new District Six – is a place without a soul ... Walk down any one of its streets and you will sense the feeling of hopelessness" *Cape Herald, The. News Mirror*, 1972. 28 October, p. 6.

between 1923 and 1931)[12] teams played each other in 1938. Each team had to provide its own ball. As a rule playing fields weren't so great and, not surprisingly, the Magnolia team's ball was lost during the match. They pleaded with Avenirs to let them use their (Avenirs') ball. The plea fell on deaf ears; Avenirs declined and advised Magnolias to find another ball. When they failed to get another ball the Avenirs team claimed the points for the incomplete match. What happened, though, was that the union, in its wisdom, overruled the decision and ordered that the match be replayed (Pick 2015:12–15).

The union also lost some of its players during the Second World War as was evidenced by a moment of silence observed as a mark of respect in memory of "Mr. J. Abrahams, member of the Avenirs Club, who had died on active service" in the Board meeting of the 10th September 1942 (Minutes of the Maitland-Parow and Districts Cricket Union, 1942). It was also reported that the Parow Cricket Club was almost excluded from the competition because its secretary had left for "active duty" and did not respond to the notice of the Annual General Meeting. This connectedness with international events is an interesting part of the history of the MPDCU.

Let's talk about more about the notion of decolonising cricket history. We know about the difficulties that prevailed in organisations and in the MPCDU we have practical examples of schisms along racial, ethnic and religious lines that manifested themselves. This was not unique to South Africa and it was visible in India and elsewhere. In India, for example, the Parsis, Hindus and expats formed their own leagues which led to multi-league tournaments (Pick 2015:18–19). The highly critically acclaimed Bollywood movie, *Lagaan*, explored the role of cricket in dismantling entrenched practices of the Indian caste system. Similarly, there were "inter-racial" cricket tournaments in South Africa until the 1950s. This arrangement was a British imperialist strategy of divide and rule. 'Racial' sport was actively encouraged by British imperialists, as reflected by the trophies they donated to sport bodies. Another aspect of the colonial link to sport was the notion of 'worthiness'. The notion of 'civilised gentlemen' is reflective of the expressions by people like Sol Plaatje[13] and Mahatma Ghandi. So the playing of the imperialists' game in itself became a statement of the colonised people's perceived worthiness. But by the 70s, cricket became part of the clarion call for opposing *apartheid* and heralded a progressive change in the notion of sport. Cricket underwent a dramatic transformation from a colonial game to a game reflective of anti-colonial activism.

There is a link between what happened in the Maitland-Parow area and what happened elsewhere. So, I want to just cogitate on a few issues that reflect the actual going on of the union.

Apartheid left an indelible impression on the organisation of cricket as it did on all forms of sport and social activities in communities and the MPCDU felt the impact of the Group Areas Act. It devastated cricket and many clubs disappeared. We have heart-rending accounts from players who experienced the brutality of the Group Areas Act (Pick 2015:23–27) and its effects on their lives and the lives of their families and neighbours.

---

12 Pick W. 2015. *One for the Chuck*, p. 8.
13 Solomon Tshekiso Plaatje (1876–1932). Plaatje was a founder member of the South African National Native Congress (later African National Congress). He involved himself in elite cultural pursuits such as the Mafekeng Philharmonic Society, Willan B. 1984. *Sol Plaatje*, p. 148.

Let us talk about family. Most of the clubs belonging to the MPCDU started by families getting together and playing the game. An example of this is the Island Rose Club founded by Frank Yon who, as mentioned earlier, played cricket with the British garrison on St. Helena Island. He moved to Cape Town and settled in Goodwood. He had seven sons and they started their own club, the Island Rose Cricket Club (Pick 2015:8). That story makes a connection between the island and cricket in the Cape and many other connections, but also indicates links between St. Helena Island, British colonialism and, indirectly, the frontier wars in the Eastern Cape. In the Yon family, women were very much part of the cricket environment, but because they were getting bored, they ended up playing softball. This was to have an adverse effect on cricket as many of the men started playing baseball, no doubt to be a closer to their female counterparts. Francois Cleophas and Floris van der Merwe have written a historical account of baseball and softball in Maitland (Cleophas & Van der Merwe 2011).

Playing conditions generally were not good. Fields were not well prepared and players were at risk of twisting an ankle in mole burrows of which there were many. Fields were nothing like what we have today. Grounds were created where there were unused pieces of land by the people themselves. Eventually Boards of Control were established to govern these grounds. However, some of these Boards were administered by collaborationist officials who took reactionary positions with regard to apartheid. They thought nothing of punishing clubs that opposed apartheid. An example was the Elsies River Cricket Club that was banned from using the cricket field for a number of seasons because they opposed the tour by a rebel West Indian team (Pick 2015:27).

The sad part of the history was the division between different groups. Cleophas and Van der Merwe (2011) reported on the contradictions in the sport colour bar. This also happened in cricket and in 1923 the Peninsula and Western Districts Cricket Board was established as a breakaway Board from the Western Province Coloured Cricket Union and formed a union of seven or eight clubs that did not allow people who were African or Muslim to join their clubs. It was an infamous rule: rule 2 of the constitution of the union. There are beautiful stories of efforts made to break down these barriers. What was striking was that within a few years of the establishment of this segregationist union there were conscientious objections by delegates of some clubs affiliated to the union about the exclusion of Africans and Muslims. However, it took ten years for that rule to be changed after repeated appeals by Mr Khan, who was a patron of the union and who provided much-needed financial support. This was in spite of the fact that as a Muslim he was not allowed to play cricket in the union. Mr Kahn's written appeals to a number of AGMs eventually led to a revision of the constitution. When this revision took place it came with some caveats. The so-called Mohamedan players had to form their own separate club and were only then allowed to play in the Maitland-Parow and Districts Cricket Union (Pick 2015:23–27). These are things that are seldom talked about as I think people are reluctant to discuss this discriminatory aspect of what was known as Non-European cricket organisation at the time.

Appropriate attire was very important in those days and was part of cricket's colonial legacy. But it also afforded the union the opportunity to penalise players for not wearing appropriate attire while playing the game. This proved to provide the union with a useful source of income. Umpiring was not a strong point in the Maitland-Parow and Districts Cricket Union and coaching was pretty much non-existent until the 1970s.

In spite of these difficulties encountered by players, the legacy is extraordinary. It produced some of the most renowned 21st century international cricketers. Players like Vernon Philander, one of the fastest bowlers in test cricket with 50 wickets to his credit and ranked number one in the world. Alphonso Thomas, one of the world's best one-day international players, Shandre Fritz, South African national women's cricket players, Shibnam Ismail, South African national women's fast bowler have ties with the MPCDU. The union also produced administrators like Percy Sonn, who served as the President of the Western Province Cricket Board, President of the South African Cricket Board and later the first African President of the International Cricket Council. Barney Leendertz occupied the position of secretary of the Western Province Cricket Board for 17 years and later became the secretary of the first United Cricket Board of South Africa. Neville Hartel, George Van Oordt, Nico Van Oordt, Gert Williams, John Neethling and many others served Western Province Cricket in a range of capacities. Wilfred Diedricks, another player from the MPCDU, served as an international umpire for years. Many clubs, currently participating in competitions in Western Province are off-springs that formed part of the MPDCU.

In conclusion, the history of the Maitland-Parow and Districts Cricket Union illustrates the link between international events and local effects, and the value of community action and self-reliance. Sport, as a feature of human endeavour, where people organise themselves as collectives and take on challenges, has the potential to produce some of the most amazing consequences for humanity.

References

Allen, D. 2008. South African Cricket, Imperial Cricketers and Imperial Expansion, 1850-1910. *The International Journal of the History of the Sport,* 25(4), March 2008:443-471. https://doi.org/10.1080/09523360701814789

Allie, M. 2000. *More than a game. History of the Western Province Cricket Board*. Cape Town: Western Province Cricket Association.

Bickford-Smith, V., Van Heyningen, E. & Worden, N. 1999. *Cape Town in the twentieth century. An illustrated social history*. Cape Town: David Phillip Publishers.

Cleophas F.J. & Van der Merwe F.J.G. 2011. Mapping out an obscured South African sport history landscape through Edward Henderson. *African Journal for Physical, Health Education, Recreation and Dance*, June, 17(2):226–238.

Cleophas F.J & Van der Merwe F.J.G. 2011. Contradictions and responses in the South African sport colour bar with special reference to the Western Cape. *African Journal for Physical, Health Education, Recreation and Dance (AJPHERD)*, March 17 (1):124-140.

Korr, C. & Close, M. 2008. *More than just a game. Soccer v Apartheid*. London: Harper-Collins Publishers.

Minutes of the Maitland-Parow and Districts Cricket Union 1942. 10 September.

Pick, W. 2015. *One for the Chuck. Glimpses into the history of the Maitland-Parow and Districts Cricket Union. 1912-1976*. Cape Town: Western Province Cricket Association.

Plaatje, S.T. 1916. *Native life in South Africa*. London: King & Son Limited.

Weeder, M. 2006. The palaces of memory. A reconstruction of District One, Cape Town, before and after the Group Areas Act. Unpublished MA mini-thesis. Bellville: University of the Western Cape.

Willan, B. 1984. *Sol Plaatje: A biography*. Berea: Ravan Press.

The interrelatedness of 'random' events: Exploring what the 'enfant terrible' child diarist Iris Vaughan, Per Henrik Ling and Danie Craven had in common

Sigi Howes

Principal at the Centre for Conservation Education, Wynberg, Cape Town,
Western Cape Education Department

As a historian, I have become increasingly fascinated by how events and people that appear to have nothing in common cross-section each other. I am currently writing a biography of the journalist and child diarist, Iris Vaughan.[1]

The *Diary of Iris Vaughan* has been in almost constant print from 1958 to 2010. Vaughan's other published works include extracts of *The Diary* in *The Adelaide Free Press* (1949–1951), *The Outspan* (1955–1956) and *Village Life* (2007); her autobiographical books *These were my Yesterdays* (1966) and *Last of the Sunlit Years* (1969); a History textbook entitled *True Stories from South Africa's History* (1931); an award-winning historical novel *O Valiant Hearts* (1984); and articles in the *Adelaide Free Press, Cape Argus, Cape Mercury, Cape Times, The Daily Dispatch, The Herald and The Cape*. In 1934 Vaughan was a founder member of the King William's Town branch of the National Council of Women (NCW). She became the editor of the Council's monthly newsletter *NCW News* (1936–1937), and was also its International Press Secretary. For her work in the NCW Vaughan was awarded the King's Coronation Medal in 1937. For all of the above reasons, she is worthy of our attention.

The childhood impulse to keep a diary is very common. However, few seem to sustain the effort; fewer are sufficiently witty, observant and lively to warrant publication (Alexander 2006:17–34). It is no surprise, then, to find that published juvenile diaries are extremely rare[2]. *The Diary of Iris Vaughan* is one such publication and the only one in South Africa. It records life in a small Karoo town in South Africa before, during and after the South African War (1899–1902), as seen through the sharp eyes of an intelligent, observant child. Generations of South African readers have been delighted by her freshness of observation, her curiosity,

---

1   Henrietta Emily Iris Vaughan (1890–1977).
2   The autobiographical writings of the Brontë children are perhaps the best known; less well- known is the childhood diary of Virginia Wolf.

her wit, her love of words, and her ability to convey character and tell a compelling story. Professor Elwyn Jenkins of the Department of English Studies at UNISA acknowledges that, despite certain shortcomings[3], *The Diary's* appeal lies in its childlike humour (2006:27). The bibliographer Denis Godfrey refers to *The Diary* as Africana and Vaughan as "the *enfant terrible* of Africana" (1963:182, 190).

Professor Peter Alexander of the School of English at the University of New South Wales in Sydney, Australia, has a scholarly interest in child autobiographies and has published several articles on Iris Vaughan.[4] He compares Vaughan's *Diary* favourably to other colonial children's writings[5] (2004:xi). It is the voice through which the child writer speaks that influenced Jeanette Eve[6] to include *The Diary of Iris Vaughan* in her book *A Literary Guide to the Eastern Cape*, maintaining that "*The Diary* remains Vaughan's masterpiece. It brings a Karoo light note, but is not without some penetrating observations of its time and place" (2003:243). In fact, so accurate are the child's remembrances of historical events - such as a Boer incursion into Maraisburg in 1901 - that the respected South African Boer War historian, Dr Taffy Shearing, includes that incident in her book *General Smuts and his long ride* (2000:63-64).

During the course of my research, I have frequently had to step sideways and interrogate topics not normally associated with Iris Vaughan. Yet her life story proves to be a tapestry of hitherto unknown strands, including Physical Education. This chapter offers a serendipitous look into how, when one researches, one's search for information sometimes leads one down other paths that one initially did not expect to travel. I look specifically at how three different individuals are unexpectedly connected in what I've called the interconnectedness 'of seemingly random things'. They are Iris Vaughan the child diarist; Per Henrik Ling[7], who is generally regarded as the 'Father of the Swedish System of Gymnastics' (Van der Merwe 2007:202); and Dr Danie Craven[8], the South African rugby player, academic, rugby coach and sports administrator.

So who was Iris Vaughan? She was born in Kenhardt, Namaqualand, in 1890 as the daughter of Cecil Roger Vaughan (1852–1924) and his wife Martha Margaretha Ackermann (1867-1947). Her father was first a magistrate's clerk, then an assistant magistrate and finally a magistrate in the Cape colonial judiciary[9] and the family moved frequently. Iris started school at Cradock in 1896, where Miss Laura Llewellyn, the daughter of Canon William Llewellyn, ran a small private school at the Rectory of the St Peter's Anglican Church. In 1897, when her father was transferred to Maraisburg, she was enrolled at the Maraisburg Public School. However, at

---

3 The absence of dates and chronological order, and the question around whether the adult Iris edited her own childhood writing.

4 Who is Iris Vaughan? New light on a remarkable colonial child autobiographer. AUMLA: Journal of the Australasian Universities Modern Language Association (105) [May 2006]. pp. 17– 34, 147. *Introduction* in the 2004 and 2010 editions of *The Diary of Iris Vaughan*. Sydney: Juvenilia Press. pp. xi–xxxv.

5 The autobiographical records of the Brontë children; the journal of Emily Shore recording her privileged childhood; the juvenile writings of John Ruskin; the childhood diary of Virginia Woolf and the journal of Opal Whiteley, a lonely little girl in an Oregon logging camp.

6 A writer and teacher from Grahamstown. In 2003, she published her book *A Literary Guide to the Eastern Cape*, which celebrates poetry and prose from about 80 authors who have written about the places, people and natural beauty of the Eastern Cape.

7 Per Henrik Ling (1776–1839)

8 Daniël Hartman Craven (1910–1993)

9 Cape of Good Hope Civil Service Lists from 1880 to 1924.

the outbreak of the South African War in 1899, she was taken out of the school and tutored privately at home, together with her younger brother, Charles. Her tutor was a Xhosa-speaking man, Robert Mateza. In 'The Diary' Mateza is referred to only as 'George', who was a translator in the Maraisburg court where her father was the magistrate. Identifying him was not easy, but he is listed in the Cape of Good Hope Civil Service Lists. He had an Elementary Teachers' Certificate from the Clarkebury Native Training Institute in the Eastern Cape, but obviously felt he could earn more money as a court interpreter. Mateza taught English Grammar and Arithmetic to the Vaughan children for a few months before he left Maraisburg. Once the Vaughans moved to Adelaide in 1902, Iris attended the Adelaide Public School (now Adelaide High School) and did her matric there in 1906. After high school she studied at Rhodes University College in Grahamstown (now Rhodes University) and taught for a short time at the Girls' Public School in East London (now Clarendon Girls' High) and at the Adelaide Public School. She married a local farmer, Leslie Niland, and had two children: Patricia Leslie Niland (1916–1969) and Wendy Iris Niland (1921–1996). Her husband died at a relatively young age and left her almost destitute. She then had to support herself and so became a freelance journalist for various Cape newspapers including the *Cape Argus*, *Cape Times*, *Cape Mercury, Daily Dispatch* and *The Herald*. But it is through her childhood writing that she became famous. The book she eventually compiled as an adult was the diary that she had kept as a child, and it was published in 1958 under the title 'The Diary of Iris Vaughan' by the Central News Agency.

This is the opening extract from that diary, and it explains why Godfrey refers to Vaughan as the 'enfant terrible' of South Africa; the precocious young writer was only seven years old at the time:

> Today is my birthday. I am going to write a diry a diray a diery Book. Pop told me I could. He gave me this fat book. It was a govenment book, but it is mine now. I shall write here in the loft and hide my book in the old box with straw where no one can see it. Every one should have a diery. Becos life is too hard with the things one must say to be perlite and the things one must not say to lie. This is something I can never get right. If I say you are an ugly old man, that is bad manners, and if I say you are not an ugly old man I am telling a lie and not speaking the truth, the whole truth and nothing but the truth so help me God. That is what the peopel say in the witnes box when they are at a case in the courthouse. When they say this it is a great sin to tell a lie. Pop says to the witnes who is to speak about the prisoner what you are to say is the truth the whole truth and nothing but the truth, and the witnes says so Help me God. Then he tells the truth and is not punished. But in our house it is not like that. The other day when Mr O was eating with us he said You are my little sweethart, and I said NO and he said Why not and I said So help me God becos you are such an ugly old man with hair on your face. For that I was sent to bed without any more dinner not even jelly and had a good jawing about perliteness. All the time I said I was only telling the truth Mom said Nonsense. you are just a rude little girl. So Pop said you can have a diary and write all the truth in it and when you cant speak the truth its better to hold your tongue. That is why I am writing. (Vaughan 2010:1–2)

The ugly old man with hair on his face did actually exist – he was James Henry Ogilvie (1825-1909), a salt farmer in Maraisburg in the Eastern Cape (now called Hofmeyr)[10]. In her diary, Iris makes mention of over 200 people by name (sometimes using a pseudonym to protect the identity of certain individuals), and it has been part of my research to correctly

---

10 He is listed in various Voters' Registers for Maraisburg between 1895 and 1899 as a salt manufacturer and manager on the farm *Varschvlei*.

identify and trace them. She writes about actual incidences that affected her young life, such as her first day at the Maraisburg Public School – the first 'big school' she had ever been to – and about which she wrote with such humour that it was sketched by the cartoonist from the *Cape Argus*, JH Jackson. I have also verified the historic incidences she wrote about – such as the laying of the foundation stone of the Queen's Central Hospital in Cradock on 22 June 1897 – and been able to prove the accuracy of this (*The Cradock Register*: 25 June 1897) and all similar events.

Much of her writing centres on her father, who was clearly the most important person in her life. One of her literary strengths is the recording of direct speech, and she spares her readers none of the eccentricity of Cecil Vaughan's explosive language and the expletives with which he punctuated it! It adds greatly to one's enjoyment of reading 'The Diary'. Cecil Vaughan was also a cricket player and is mentioned in Luckin's book on the history of cricket in South Africa (Luckin 1915:19, 139, 141, 142, 155, 177, 179, 180, 483 and 486). Vaughan captained the Standard Cricket Club in Cradock, played in the Champion Bat Tournament, the forerunner of the Currie Cup and started by the Port Elizabeth municipality in 1876 (Odendaal 2003:41). There is a photograph and mention of Vaughan in the Western Province Cricket Club in Newlands. The Champion Bat Tournament was started by the Port Elizabeth municipality in 1876 (Odendaal 2003:41).

Iris was a good sportswoman herself: she played hockey and tennis, as mentioned several times in 'The Diary', and she appears in a 1905 photograph when drill was introduced at the Adelaide Public School under the instructorship of Sergeant Jackson, newly retired from the SA War. Ex-military types were considered desirable for the teaching of Physical Culture as many of the exercises were based on military exercises such as marching. She also played tennis for the Rhodes University College in 1911 (Currey 1970: photo facing p. 35).

The 'Diary of Iris Vaughan' was a South African bestseller from the time it was first published in serial form in the *Outspan* magazine of 1955 and 1956, and then in book form in 1958 by the Central News Agency. It appealed largely to a white, English-speaking adult readership, more so than to children. It was not generally known to the Afrikaans-speaking population, never having been translated into any other language. There were at the time of its publication in the 1950s, people alive who remembered Vaughan as a little girl always writing; many letters to the editor of the *Outspan* attested to this (*The Outspan*: 1955:2 December, 16 December; 1956: 6 January, 20 January, 24 February, 2 March, 9 March, 16 March, 13 April & 29 June).

As mentioned, Iris had two daughters. Both studied teaching, specialising in Physical Culture. Of interest to this chapter is the elder daughter, Patricia Niland. After matriculating in 1933 at the Convent of the Sacred Heart in King William's Town, she did her basic teacher training at the King William's Town Training College (founded in 1914). She qualified in 1935 with a Primary Teachers' Certificate (*Education Gazette* 3 February 1936:135). In 1936 she enrolled at the Cape Town Training College (founded in 1894) for a two-year course in Physical Culture which had been introduced in 1921 (Goodwin 1983:103), specialising in the Swedish Gymnastics founded by Per Henrik Ling. The major components of the course were Swedish Drill (apparatus work and exercises), Musical Drill, School Games and Class Teaching on the practical side; and Anatomy, Physiology, Hygiene and the Theory of Gymnastics and Games, as well as Psychology (Goodwin:104). Her lecturers included Margeret Black (who was in charge of the Physical Culture Department at the College), Anna Stegmann Anders (who later became the Principal of the King William's Town Training College) and Mrs Alison

Salmon (Staff List 1936). Alison Salmon later became the co-ordinator and inspector for Physical Culture in the then Orange Free State, and was a close personal friend of Patricia's.

But because the College dropped the second year of the Physical Culture course at the end of 1936 (Goodwin 1983:104), Niland qualified at the end of that year with a Higher Certificate (*Education Gazette*, 6 February 1937:175) instead of the Full Physical Culture Certificate she had hoped to achieve. In 1937 she therefore enrolled at the Normal School[11] in Pretoria to do that second year (Vaughan 1966:141; estimate of date mine). The Normal School had been founded in 1902, and in 1954 became the Pretoria Teachers' College. In 1938 Niland accepted a teaching post in Physical Education at the Normal School (Vaughan 1966:154; estimation of date mine). In July 1939 she was invited by the then Transvaal Education Department to be part of a South African delegation under the leadership of Danie Craven to attend a massive display of gymnastics in Stockholm, Sweden, to celebrate the 100th anniversary of Ling's death. Dubbed the 'Lingiad', it attracted 7 399 gymnasts from 37 countries; more than the number of athletes at the 1936 Olympic Games in Berlin. Patricia Niland was probably selected on the strength that she was one of the most highly trained Physical Education lecturers in South Africa at the time. In addition to attending the 'Lingiad', the team was also deputised to visit Belgium, Denmark, Germany, Great Britain and Holland afterwards to study the latest Physical Education methods in those countries (*Cape Mercury* 28 June 1939), but the outbreak of World War II in August 1939 prevented this.

That brings me to the second person in this equation: Per Henrik Ling. He was a Swede and a teacher of modern languages; he wrote poetry and became interested in gymnastics when he took up fencing and some milder forms of sport, which cured his joint pain. He consequently made a study of gymnastics (Siedentop 1990:29). Ling didn't believe so much in sport at a competitive level; the type of gymnastics that he worked on was more along the lines of mass participation, good posture, and health and fitness. Early in the 19th century Ling emphasised running, jumping, fencing and swimming in his programme. By 1820 he had devised free-standing exercises that had to be performed according to anatomical principles, i.e. exercises for every body part, but executed separately (Postma 1945:83). Ling particularly advocated his system in four different branches – the pedagogical, medical, aesthetic and military aspects – the latter will be of particular interest when I come to the third protagonist, Danie Craven.

Ling's movements were very fluid, and women and even elderly men were not excluded. Even young children could do Swedish gymnastics. The co-operative nature of it won mass appeal and the system spread throughout the world, particularly in Europe. It was through Great Britain that the Lingian system came to South Africa. Much has been written about Ling, although only a few local researchers have dealt with the historical development of the Lingian system in South Africa (Cleophas 2009 & Willemse 1969). Ling is frequently referred to as 'the father of modern gymnastics' and although his methodology has been replaced by more modern methods, the theory and aesthetics of it still forms part of modern gymnastics today.

The last person to be discussed in this account is Danie Craven. He was an academic, a rugby player, a rugby coach and a sports administrator. He studied at Stellenbosch University

---

11 'Normal' in this context does not have anything to do with the opposite of abnormal – it refers to norms and standards and was a way of standardising the training of teachers.

between 1929 and 1935, earning his first PhD in 1935[12]. He then went on to teach for a while; one of the schools he taught at was St Andrew's College in Grahamstown. While there, he was selected to play for the Springbok rugby team. He played 16 tests for the Springboks as scrumhalf between 1931 and 1938. In 1938 he joined the Union Defence Force (UDF) as Director of Physical Education, where he was responsible for creating a physical training division. After the Second World War he became the national rugby selector and Springbok coach from 1949 to 1956. He was elected president of the South African Rugby Board in 1956 and was president of the unified South African Rugby Football Union at the time of his death in 1993. It was while he was in the UDF that Craven came to be appointed as the leader of the South African delegation to Europe in 1939 to study the Swedish gymnastics that Ling had developed, given that Ling advocated its application to the military as was previously mentioned.

In 1939 – from 20 July to 4 August – the Swedish Gymnastics Federation organised a large get-together in Stockholm for gymnasts from all over the world to celebrate the 100th anniversary of the death of Per Ling. Loosely named the 'Lingiad', it was attended by over 7,000 gymnasts from 37 countries who participated in it, more than the number for the 1936 Berlin Olympic Games. The German team was one of the biggest and its gymnasts enthralled the audience with their displays. The appearance of the Women's League of Health and Beauty was also wildly cheered. In 1930, a woman driven by British ideas on race, Mary Bagot Stack, had founded the League. She articulated her self-confessed aim as "cultivating 'racial health'". This she based on her belief that health and beauty helped to furnish peace after the devastation of World War I. Her ideas regenerated British national pride and the cultivation of health, youth and vigour during the inter-war years (Connolly & Einzig 1987:189). I can remember my own mother participating in the Women's League of Health and Beauty in Cape Town in the 1970s.

A programme for the Lingiad was published, listing all the participating countries and delegates, as well as the events. On page 2 of this programme, Danie Craven's name as the head of the South African delegation, appears. But there was also a conference on Physical Education after the display of the games, and listed as one of the delegates to the conference was the afore-mentioned Patricia Niland, with the designation 'gymnastics teacher'. And that is how three unlikely candidates were brought together in one event.

As a researcher, it is immensely gratifying when looking at one form of research as I did, starting with Iris Vaughan, to end up with someone like Danie Craven, because there does not appear to be any commonality. But as a historian I am constantly finding new ways of linking incidents and people who, on the surface, appear to be unrelated but are so often interrelated.

---

[12]   A further two followed in 1973 and 1979.

The publication (Central News Agency, 1958) that made Iris Vaughan famous. The cover drawing by the well-known cartoonist, JH Jackson, alludes to the light-hearted content of the book.

Iris Vaughan, third from the right in the back row in an Edwardian drill class at the Adelaide Public School in 1905. The other two girls with dots on their collars are her sisters Florence and Gwyneth. Later her daughters would follow suit and become Physical Education lecturers. The instructor, Sergeant Jackson, is at centre back. Dumbbells were a relatively new phenomenon at the time (original photo in the private collection of Sean Pretorius, Iris Vaughan's grandson).

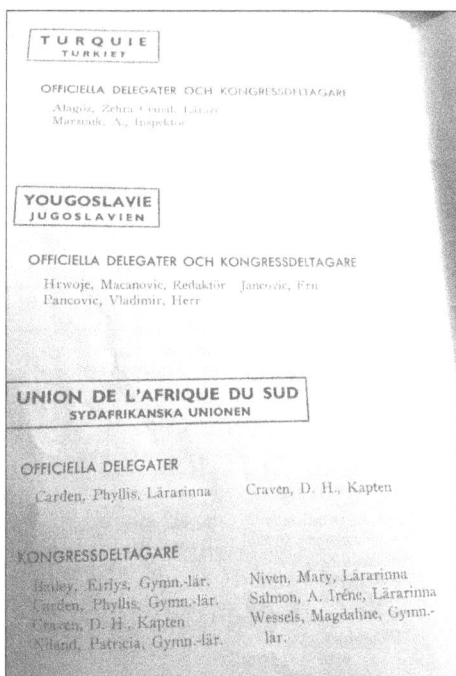

TURQUIE
TURKIET

OFFICIELLA DELEGATER OCH KONGRESSDELTAGARE
Alagöz, Zehra Cemal, Lärare
Marzouk, A., Inspektör

YOUGOSLAVIE
JUGOSLAVIEN

OFFICIELLA DELEGATER OCH KONGRESSDELTAGARE
Hrwoje, Macanovic, Redaktör   Jancovic, Frn
Pancovic, Vladimir, Herr

UNION DE L'AFRIQUE DU SUD
SYDAFRIKANSKA UNIONEN

OFFICIELLA DELEGATER
Carden, Phyllis, Lärarinna   Craven, D. H., Kapten

KONGRESSDELTAGARE
Bailey, Eirlys, Gymn.-lär.   Niven, Mary, Lärarinna
Carden, Phyllis, Gymn.-lär.   Salmon, A. Iréne, Lärarinna
Craven, D. H., Kapten   Wessels, Magdaline, Gymn.-
Niland, Patricia, Gymn.-lär. lär.

Patricia Niland and Danie Craven listed as part of the South African delegation at to the 1939 Lingiad (photo: Francois Cleophas)

Birthplace of Per Henrik Ling in Småland, Sweden (photo: Francois Cleophas)

References

Alexander, P.F. 2006. Who is Iris Vaughan? New light on a remarkable colonial child autobiographer. *AUMLA: Journal of the Australasian Universities Modern Language Association*, (105) [May 2006].

Bale, S. 1993. 'Obituary: Danie Craven'. London: *The Independent*.

Cape of Good Hope Civil Service Lists for 1880, 1881, 1882, 1883, 1884, 1885 and 1886. Cape Town: Saul Solomon & Co.

Cape of Good Hope Civil Service Lists for 1887 and 1888. Cape Town: J.C. Juta & Co.

Cape of Good Hope Civil Service Lists for 1889 1924: Cape Town: W.A. Richards & Sons.

Cleophas, F.J. 2009. Physical education and physical culture in the Coloured community of the Western Cape, 1837–1966. Unpublished PhD dissertation. Stellenbosch: Stellenbosch University.

Connolly, C. & Einzig, H. 1987. *The fitness jungle. Stage 2 fitness: The exercise survival guide*. London: Century Hutchinson.

Currey, R.F. 1970. *Rhodes University, 1904–1970. A Chronicle*. Grahamstown: Rhodes University.

Eve, J. 2003: *A Literary Guide to the Eastern Cape. Places and the Voices of Writers*. Cape Town: Double Storey.

Godfrey, D. 1963. *The Enchanted Door. A discourse on Africana book-collecting, with notes on famous collectors, collections and books. Chapter 14: A Child's Remarkable Diary*. Cape Town: Howard Timmins.

Goodwin, A.R. 1983. Cape Town Training College. 1894–1937. Unpublished research essay submitted in partial fulfilment of the requirements for the degree of BA Honours in History at the University of Cape Town. Cape Town: University of Cape Town.

Howes, S. 2008-2018. The Life and Times of Iris Vaughan. Unpublished biography.

Jenkins, E. 2006. *The National Character in South African English Children's Literature*. New York: Routledge & Francis Taylor Group. https://doi.org/10.4324/9780203943922

'"King" Physical Culturalists', *The Cape Mercury*, 28 June 1939, King William's Town.

Luckin, M.W. 1915. *The History of South African Cricket. Including the full scores of all important matches since 1876*. Johannesburg: W.E. Hortor & Co.

Odendaal, A. 2003. *The Story of an African Game: Black Cricketers and the Unmasking of One of South Africa's Greatest Myths*, 1850–2003. Cape Town: David Phillip Publishers.

Postma, J.W. 1945. Ondersoek na die wetenskaplike basis van die Europese strominge in die liggaamsopvoeding van 1900 tot 1940 (Investigation into the scientific basis of the European streams in physical education from 1900 to 1945). Unpublished DEd dissertation. Stellenbosch: Stellenbosch University.

Records of the Cape Town Training College from 1895 to 1994 held at the Education Museum, Wynberg, Western Cape (including the Staff List quoted in this paper).

Shearing, T. & D. 2000. *General Smuts and his long ride. Cape Commando Series No. 3*. Sedgefield: Taffy & David Shearing.

Siedentop, D. 1990. *Introduction to physical education, fitness and sport*. London: Mayfield Publishers.

The Cradock Register. Government Gazette for the Division of Cradock. Friday 25 June 1897. Cradock: H.E. Turkington.

The Education Gazette of the Province of the Cape of Good Hope, Vol XXXV, No. 2, 3 February 1936. Cape Town: Department of Public Education.

The Education Gazette of the Province of the Cape of Good Hope, Vol XXXVI, No. 3, 6 February 1937. Cape Town: Department of Public Education.

Treharne, M. 1948. *The History of the National Council of Women of South Africa 1909–1948*. Cape Town: National Council of Women of South Africa. Archives and Manuscripts, University of Cape Town Libraries: Ref 2: WN2:65/1.

Van der Merwe, F.J.G. 2007. *Sport history. A handbook for South African students*. Stellenbosch: F.J.G. Publications.

Vaughan, I. 1966. *These Were My Yesterdays*. Cape Town: Howard Timmins.

Vaughan, I. 2010. *The Diary of Iris Vaughan*. Sydney: Juvenilia Press. Revised edition by Peter F. Alexander, Peter Midgley and Sigi Howes.

Willemse J.J. 1969. Die invloed van die Sweedse stelsel van formele oefeninge op die ontwikkeling van liggaamlike opvoeding in Suid-Afrika (The system of formal exercises on the development of Physical Education in South Africa). Unpublished MA thesis. Potchefstroom: Potchefstroom University for Christian Higher Education.

The establishment [white] media played a pivotal role in the marginalisation and ignorance of non-racial sport and its achievers during apartheid, thereby keeping whites and the international sports fraternity in the dark. Unless a black sport code had a sympathetic reporter [in black or white media], that sport enjoyed little newspaper coverage and depended only on recollections, private records, result sheets minutes, etc. to preserve its history. Today, a large section of local media perpetuates this past and still ignores historical perspectives on black sports achievements. This chapter argues that recognition and honouring of past black non-racial cycling heroes can come about through social media reporting. This is correct because financial support for research and publication about South African non-racial cycling history is lacking unless it is part of formal academic research. Within this historical context, various websites and Facebook sites have been initiated to give recognition and credit to black sport heroes by honouring them as role models, beyond the present-day popular heroes.

Introduction

South African blacks in Cape Town have an organisational cycling history that stretches back to 1898 when the Good Hope Athletic Club (Coloured) was founded. This notwithstanding, the [white] sport media in South Africa continue to ignore this rich legacy and in so doing, contribute to its silencing and marginalisation. In the past it was left to a few black reporters, working for the white media houses, to provide a semblance of reporting. Given the limited capacity to cover all or most of the sports code nationally, very little public records or archives are available. Present-day historians are therefore forced to rely on personal recollections and small and fragmented private archives in order to create decolonised narratives.

Popular works on cycling display an unashamedly white bias. Prime examples of these are: *Die Paarl se Boxing Day Sports* (Human 1984); *Centenary: 100 years of organised South African cycling racing* (Jowett 1981); *The cycle tour* (Wills 2008); *The world's greatest cycle tour* (Camplin 2012); *The World's Greatest Cycle Tour* (Brink 2017). There is also a dearth of public archived information on South African non-racial or black cycling history, at a time that there is a strong official drive to recognise past heroes as part of the process to promote nation-building and reconciliation. Therefore, in the absence of documented and archived statistics, how does one contribute to decolonial discourses on South African non-racial cycling history? I ask myself the same question as Morgan Ndlovu did, when he wrote on decolonisation within another context: "To what extent has past patterns of inventing and packaging history for disunity and domination been reversed and re-directed towards the attainment of an inclusive common belonging by the postcolonial and post-apartheid governments?" (Ndlovu 2016:9). I agree with Ndlovu that this question is quite important because "the cumulative effect of divisive invented historical knowledge can render it a structural constraint upon which new articulations of historical knowledge fall into the trap of repeating the same divisive knowledge even if the context has changed to that of seeking inclusive nationbuilding" (Ndlovu 2016:9). With this in mind, I proceed without an overemphasis on statistical records but instead, foregrounding a personal non-racial narrative of cycling in South Africa.

It is rather difficult to determine exactly when cycling as a sport started amongst black cyclists. What is clear however is that the expense to compete in the sport did not deter them even though they were always at a disadvantage to whites insofar as social-economic standards are concerned. This explains the lesser extent of black participation compared with whites. Lesser black participation does in no sense reflect a lack of competitiveness as sports journalist, Arrie Joubert, suggests in an article in the *Cycling Herald* of August 1964: "... non-white cycling in South Africa progressed well this year ... but our White cycling made great strides [so that] that currently a big gap exists between the two...".

The first known cycling club to date in South Africa was the Port Elizabeth Bicycle Club, formed in October 1881, and the SA Amateur Cycling Union was founded in 1892 in Johannesburg – staging its first Championships on 9 September 1893. The Paarl District Cycling club was formed in 1895 and obtained an ostrich camp from Dr A.L de Jager's Paarl Sporting Grounds Company to build a cycling track in the Western Cape. The first combined athletics and cycling meeting in Paarl was held in Paarl on 2 January 1897 and was a major success (Arendse 2012:63). It is not certain whether blacks participated in this meeting but this event led to the famous Boxing Day meeting on 26 December that year and there was no black participation. Though Paarl became accepted as the 'mecca of Coloured cycling' and boasted a number of clubs (Wanderers, Metropolitan and Swifts), it was the Yorkshire club that turns 100 in 2019, that became the pride of Paarl and the Boland during (and after) the SACOS period.

The Yorkshire Athletics and Cycling club was formed in 1919 in Maitland by Thomas, Edward and Danie Daniëls, Pitre and Charlie Ockert, and Charlie Blows, together with a few race walkers. When Mr Cupido (Kiepie) Green settled in Paarl in the late 1930s, the Yorkshire club was also established there. The name 'Yorkshire' stems from the material of cycling jerseys which was imported from the English county Yorkshire. Mr Green became a legend in Paarl because of his achievements between 1930 and 1950. Once, after riding from Paarl to Kimberley, he won most of his events at the De Beers track (Arendse, 2012:65-66).

Two cycling bodies were affiliated at different times to the SACOS – (South African Council on Sport),[1] The South African Cycling Association (SACA) was established in the late 1960s

---

[1]   Established in on 17 March 1978 in Durban under the presidency of Norman Middleton, vice-presidency of Hassan Howa and M.N. Pather as secretary. The SACOS's initial aim was to oppose the government's multi-national sport policy and to provide non-racial participation opportunities to South Africans.

according to Mr Chesssie Pieterse, cyclist and son of one of the presidents, Mr Peter Pieterse. The South African Cycling Board (SACB) was established in 1978. The SACA was led at various times by presidents Peter Pieterse (Boland); Edgar Rhoda (Griqualand West) and Japie Green. Mr Pieterse, a school teacher, lived in Worcester and was also involved with the Boland rugby union. His sons and one daughter all participated in cycling – Chesterton [Chessie] being the national sprint champion for some years and his sister Patty being one of the first black women cyclists in South Africa. Rhoda was a businessman from Kimberley, who owned some pharmacies and was involved with the Labour Party.[2]

Japie Green was a businessman who owned his own successful plumbing business in Paarl and was a member of the famous Green cycling family. His brother Cupido (Cippie) was a formidable road and track cyclist in South Africa. Cippie's son, Kevin, was one of the first black junior Springboks when the SACA affiliated to the S.A. Cycling Federation in 1977.

The South African Cycling Association (SACA) took a majority decision in 1977 that their cyclists should exit the SACOS fold and join the multi-racial South African Cycling Federation (SACF). The SACB wanted to provide and secure continued participation opportunities for cyclists who would not join the SACF. Cyclists who resisted the decision of their mother body, SACA, to join forces with the SACF, stopped their cycling career instead of forsaking their principled stand against multiracial cycling. The SACOS – whose policies forbade sport contacts of its members with non-SACOS-affiliated structures – then suspended the SACA and accepted the SACB as its affiliate. The SACB had, at various times, as presidents Ivan Williams (a businessman from Cape Town), Prof Ihron Rensburg (a Port Elizabeth political activist during the 80s and pharmacist – later, vice-chancellor of the University of Johannesburg) – and myself, Charles Beukes (anti-apartheid sports activist from Worcester and college lecturer). The Beukes family was heavily involved in cycling. My father, John, was the chairman of the Boland Cycling Union; my sister, Juanita Beets, served the national and regional bodies in secretarial positions while my brother, Theo, was a formidable cyclist with SACA and SACB.

The CSA president from 2012 till 2018 was William Newman, a product of the SACB. He comes from a family in Cape Town with a rich cycling tradition of administrators and champion track and road cyclists. His brothers, Brian and Edmund, were both provincial cyclists and junior national champions while his uncles, Willie and Reggie Cloete, counted amongst the elite of the non-racial cycling fraternity.

Within this historical context, various websites and Facebook sites and groups, such as *Cycling Memoirs*, *Athletics Clipboard*, *Images of SARU Legends* and *SACOS – No normal sport in an abnormal society*, *Forgotten legends of Yorkshire Cycling club's history*, have been initiated to give recognition and credit to previously SACOS-affiliated cyclists by honouring them as role models. This chapter presents a case for creating a decolonisation narrative that recognises and honours non-racial cycling heroes through the use of media, and in particular, social media.

---

2   The Labour Party of South Africa was established in 1965 with the intention of participating in the Coloured Representative Council. Coetzer, P. 1984. *Awaiting trial: Allan Hendrickse.* (Alberton: Librarius Felicitas), p. 62.

Becoming a black sport reporter

In addition to black South Africans suffering colonial and post-colonial domination in sport, they also experienced the same in the field of knowledge production about their sport participation (Ndlovu 2013:1). In the apartheid era, the establishment media ignored non-racial sport and today they still perpetuate it. I have first-hand experience of this.

I joined the Worcester Cycling club in 1970, the same year that South Africa was expelled from the International Cycling Union, and became a volunteer reporter for cycling. In 1974 I became an administrator for cycling and cycled myself. I joined the SACA, a SACOS affiliate at the time, as a freelance reporter. Sports affiliates of the SACOS committed themselves to fighting racist sport and operated under the slogan "No normal sports in an abnormal society". I was part of the formation of the first cycling club at the University of the Western Cape (UWC) in 1974. The UWC Cycling Club was the first black university club in South Africa with myself as chairman. Other founder member included Gregory Prinsloo, Fred van Wyk and Peter Malgas. This club was affiliated to the SACOS. The SACOS would have nothing to do with the efforts of white sport federations.

The establishment media was controlled by whites and did not give media exposure to SACOS-affiliated cycling events in the same manner as its coverage of white events. Mainstream white newspapers started supplements – labelled 'Extra' – and these covered SACOS cycling events. The official justification for these supplementary newspapers was that they offered the opportunity for 'more and better' coverage of events in black communities. This however created a situation that unless white readers at that time made a special effort to find the 'Extra' newspapers, they would not know what was happening in non-racial sports. White cycling supporters, administrators and participants were able to tell one everything about their Boxing Day Sport, about the Paarl Tour, the Rapport Cycle Tour[3] but they had no informed idea and knowledge on what was happening in regard to cycling in the townships. Therefore, when unification talks were taking place during the 1990s, sport administrators on the establishment side were astonished and flabbergasted when they realised how well organised, well attended and well supported sport was in the black areas. In fact, black sport lovers were far more informed about what was happening in white sport than the other way round. There were these journalists writing for these 'Extra' newspapers who did their utmost to showcase SACOS cycling. Ironically, while the 'Extra' supplements were apartheid-based and thus politically rejected by most blacks, it was a lifeline held out to them by keeping supporters, administrators and participants informed and updated. However, the names and achievements of many non-racial cyclists are lost because at the time that unification was achieved there was no SACOS affiliate to merge with the establishment South African Cycling Federation – hence the matter of unification and transformation never entered the national cycling agenda at the time.

It is against this background and historical context that websites and Facebook sites and groups have been initiated to give recognition and credit to heroes by honouring them as role models for local communities. There are social media site administrators who ventured into the history making of non-racial sports. This brought me to the theme of my article here,

---

[3]   According to the sports historian Lappe Laubscher, the idea for this 1 600 km multiday race grew out of a 1972 conversation between Arrie Joubert, a sports journalist, Raoul de Villiers, a Bloemfontein carpet merchant, and vice-chairperson of the SACF, Sean O' Toole, 'Apartheid was the spoke in South African cycling', *Mail & Guardian*, 2013.

namely that social media sites are accessible and available modes for recognising achievers from the non-racial SACOS era (1973 – c.1994).

When South African sport unified (or was consumed by) establishment sport in the 1990s, some effort was made by the South African Rugby Union (SARU)[4] to recognise achievers from the SACOS fold in rugby by offering them Springbok colours. The mainstream media did not quite know how to handle the awarding of all of these honorary colours to blacks. When they wrote sports-historical or sports-contextual articles, they referred to Springboks – meaning white apartheid-era Springboks – but excluded those [honorary/symbolic] Springboks. In my opinion, the awarding of honorary Springbok colours has not moved beyond symbolic gesturing. This doesn't auger well for those propagating the Springbok as a unifying symbol in the democratic South Africa and makes it a divisive rather than a unifying factor. The social media site, *Cycling memoirs,* was created on 23 January 2016 to give cyclists from the nonracial SACOS fold, who were active during apartheid, a showroom to post pictures, newspaper clippings etc. as recognition of their contribution to help build the sport of cycling in South Africa. William Newman, as president of Cycling South Africa, prioritised the recognition of achievers and achievements of SACOS affiliated (1977 till c.1994) and SACA (prior to 1977) cyclists. To this end a Task Group, consisting of representatives from both black cycling bodies, met with Cycling South Africa (CSA) in December 2015 in Bellville to devise a plan of action. Newman emphasised the importance of this in each presidential address. Newman, who was a cyclist at the time when I was president of the SACB, co-opted myself and Pierre Leukes (from SACA) to serve on the national executive of Cycling SA as part of the transformation agenda that would eventually include the recognition awards. Leukes was a teacher and insurance agent, and later full-time secretary of the Cape Professional Teachers Association (CPTA).[5] He served the SACA as Honorary Secretary. Leukes declined his nomination for personal reasons but continued as a member of the Task Group. A big question was how to determine standards for recognition. In sports like cycling and athletics, it is individual achievement that counts. It was however my attending of a funeral service of a SACOS cycling legend, Jackson Jantjies, that really moved me to start a social media site that would aim to record and document the achievers and achievements of non-racial cycling.

Starting a Social Media Site for Non-Racial Cycling

Funeral services became a rallying point for me in remembering non-racial sport heroes.[6] Former SACOS cycling legend Jackson Jantjies' funeral in 2015 motivated me to start 'Cycling Memoirs', where we put up pictures and stories and newspaper cuttings. Over the past three years I had realised that social media sites should not only represent the beacons of light during the darkest days of oppression, forgetting their daily toil against an unjust and oppressive regime, but that they could also revitalise and regain forgotten memories in days to come. A wall of memory, derived from information from a social media site, could thus serve as a rallying point around which to reflect nonracial sport issues.

---

4   The SA Rugby Union was established in March 1992.
5   This was a Coloured organisation that grew out of the merger of two associations: The Teachers Educational Professional Association (TEPA) and the Cape Teachers' Association (CTA).
6   During the 1990s funerals were gathering points for anti-apartheid mobilisation, see Manenzhe J. 2007, The politicisation of funerals in South Africa during the 20th century (1900–1994).

I attended the funeral service with Oom Ben Saunders of Worcester. Ben Saunders was a blue collar worker who, as a 14-year-old, initiated a rugby club with some friends to help channel the energy of his peers away from gangsterism and into constructive recreation.[7] Oom Ben was a cycling sprint champion and the only living founding member of a rugby club, Young Hamiltons (established 1948), which was named after Hamiltons Rugby Club[8] in Cape Town. This year, 2018, they are celebrating their 70th anniversary. Oom Ben started the club when he was 14 years old. This club is today still bringing much joy to the community in Worcester. Fortunately, it has a Facebook site that informs the world about its existence. Oom Ben Saunders and fellow cyclist, Willie Cloete from Cape Town, tell how they had had to train 'illegally' on tracks like Boland Park in Worcester and Green Point in Cape Town, fearing harassment from the respective municipal authorities. Saunders had to train in the dark after climbing over the fence at Boland Park to train for the 1964 SA Non White Games in Pretoria while Cloete's white training partner, Ernie Dawson, retired from cycling in dismay when Cloete was denied use of the Green Point Track for training.

Jantjies' history is equally sad. He was buried out of the Congregational Church in Paarl, where he resided. He travelled to Saldanha[9] early on Monday mornings to be at work and come back on Fridays on his bicycle. He received an offer to go overseas for coaching, but could not find someone to sponsor him. On the same day of Jackson Jantjies's funeral, it was also the funeral service for Thinus Linee[10] and I was driving past on the Klein Drakenstein Road in Paarl. I went past the Church where the Thinus Linee funeral was taking place and there was massive interest. The Mayor of Cape Town was there, the Premier was there. There were a lot of high-ranking people attending the funeral for Thinus Linee. In all respects he deserved it; he was a Springbok rugby player.

Lower down in the same street, was the venue for the funeral of Jackson Jantjies. It was the people close to him and those who knew him, and us, the SACOS cycling fraternity who attended it. It struck me that this guy, like Linee, was a champion in his sport. He could have been a Springbok cyclist at the time; could have gone overseas if he had had the opportunity and the funding but he was not given a chance. From the time of his funeral until today he has not received any official recognition. Neither the Mayor of Paarl nor of Drakenstein was there to give honour to one of its high-achieving inhabitants.

My mission in getting a Facebook page up and running is to collect data that will reverse this amnesia and dislodge notions that blacks do not have a cycling history. We do not have resources, skills and acumen to publish books, but as long as people can go to social media and keep track of what has happened in the past, I am sure that it will contribute towards decolonising non-racial perspectives through cycling.

---

7   This was a feature of the 20th century club movement. The formation of the Accro Physical Culture Club in District Six in 1933 was stimulated by a local politician, Ismail Brown, whose father encouraged him to "do something good for the local boys", Cleophas F. 2009. Physical education and physical culture in the Coloured community of the Western Cape. Unpublished PhD dissertation (Stellenbosch: Stellenbosch University), p. 209.

8   Hamiltons Rugby Club was established in 1875 by Bishops School Old Boys.

9   Depending on one of three routes, it is a distance of between 158 and 175 kilometres.

10 Linee made his provincial debut for Western Province in 1992 and played 112 games for the province until his retirement in 2001. He played in the unified rugby structure and not in the SACOS era.

TIMELINE OF BLACK CYCLING HISTORY IN SOUTH AFRICA

Date	Event
1870	Pietermaritzburg businessman imported first bicycles into South Africa
1888	A group of cyclists ride with their penny-farthings from Port Elizabeth to Cape Town
1892	The SA Amateur Cycling Union was founded and coordinated the activities of white cyclists in Johannesburg
1893	9 September 1893 hosting of the first SA Championships in Johannesburg
1894	SA Amateur Athletics and Cycling Association (white) formed on 26 March at the Wanderers in Johannesburg
1896	The *Warwick Argus* (8 August): "Ladies are taking to cycling freely, and so are educated Kaffirs. When Kaffirs that are not educated follow suit, what a splendid market for wheels in South Africa there will be!"
1897	The SAACU boasted 39 affiliated clubs nation-wide; Cape Town-based firm Donald Menzies & Co manufactured the Springbuck bicycle
1897	Green Point Cycle Track opened
1897	26 December, first Boxing Day Event in Paarl
1898	The *Evening Post* (New Zealand, 5 November) noted: "A photograph recently received from South Africa shows a Matabele damsel not heavily handicapped by clothing, calmly seated on a bicycle of the latest pattern. Kaffir kraals constitute the background of the picture, making sharper the contrast between modern civilization and ancient savagery."
1899	*The Wellington Times* (N.Z., 7 December): under the headline "Cycling in Kruger's land" noted: "Amongst the Native races in Africa cycling is fast becoming a positive rage. This is particularly so in South Africa. The Kaffirs are enthusiastic, and in King William's Town and Graham's Town they have clubs of their own. In Natal there are three native clubs. A little time ago, two blacks invested in bicycles and started careering about the streets of Johannesburg, till an industrious constable knocked them off their machines and took them into custody. There was no imprisonment inflicted on them for daring to imitate their white neighbours, but they were told that cycling was for white people not for blacks."
1899	Anglo-Boer War started. Bicycles in Johannesburg commandeered by British forces
1901	Establishment of the Western Province Amateur Athletics & Cycling Association (Coloured)
1902	The *Traralgon Record* (Victoria, Australia) noted: "Cycling is a very favorable pastime here, both amongst British, Boer and Kaffir, and would indeed make the mouths of some of the Melbourne manufacturers water to see the number of cycles in use. Bicycle shops do a splendid trade, both in sales and repairs".

Date	Event
	The Press (New Zealand) under the heading "Gossip from Johannesburg" noted: "Johannesburg is another Christchurch as far as regards its number of cycling votaries are concerned. The inhabitants would need to have the wheel in general use to support the number of cycle shops there are. All the principal streets would appear to have three or four establishments. The machines in use are almost exclusively of English make, the well-known American makes, such a favourite in New Zealand, not appearing to have a representative. Second-hand machines are very cheap."
1904	*The Evening Star* (Australia) 14 September report: "Pretoria Municipal authorities adopted a 'Kaffir Bicycle' by-law that requires all bicycles belonging to Non-Whites to be painted yellow in order to control theft."
1905	The SAACU and the SA Athletics Union merged to form the SA Amateur Athletics & Cycling Association
1908	South Africa represented by four cyclists at the Olympic Games in London
1909	The *APO* newspaper (24 May) under heading "Of European Descent" noted: "the Cape Colony Amateur Athletic and Cycling Union has introduced a system of licensing all competitors. In the form of application for a license, the applicant makes a declaration as to his amateur status, in which he has to declare that he is "of European parentage". It is remarkable that such a phrase should have been introduced into such a document. For cyclists have long had to take out licenses, and some of the most brilliant exponents of our cycling world are Coloured. Further, the Western Province Union that controls athletics in this part of the Colony includes one coloured delegate, while one, at least, of the ruling authorities in the Transvaal cycling world is undoubtedly coloured."
1909	*APO* newspaper (11 September) reported sports meeting held by the Paarl Amateur Athletic and Cycling Club 'on the Main Road from Paarl to Wellington', included cycling. Included were a One Mile Cycle Race (scratch) won by F.C. Sameuls. Two Miles Cycle (scratch) won by F.C. Sameuls
1910	Diamond Fields Cycling Club Kimberley held a road race on a Sunday morning. A. Bartes won with AE Sam a good second and Tom Boelhana third. First prize was a silver medal presented by H. Le Sar, 2nd prize silver presented by H. Michael. (*APO*, 'Athletics' 16/7/1910), p. 11
1910	Diamond Fields Cycling Club elected new office-bearers: President; N. Odes; Chairman MJ Richards; Vice-Chairman: AE Sam; Honorary Secretary: HG Blassoples; Assistant-Secretary: Peter Malander
1910	Ten-mile Handicap Bicycle Race ran under the auspices of the Rose Sporting and Empire Cycling Clubs on 16 December
1913	Ted Stevens set a 100 mile roads record for Coloured SA riders according to *APO* newspaper, 23/8/1913, p. 11
1913	Diamond Fields Coloured Cycling Club hosted annual 40 mile road race for Richards Cup on the Schmidtsdrift Road, Kimberley, won by Cecil Kinnear followed by Peter Malander and Fred Beely according to APO newspaper 8 November 1913; p. 11
1930	The *Cape Times* noted the presence of cyclist racing around a Johannesburg single-sex mine compound.

Date	Event
1946	Establishment of the SA Amateur Athletics & Cycling Board of Control (SAAACB), black national body under the leadership of J.B. Eksteen
1947	First Inter-provincial athletics and cycling meeting of the SAAACB held in Paarl Sports Ground
1948	British Team visited South Africa, first-ever overseas visit, one test in Kimberley won by the visitors
1958	SA Cycling Federation established after a breakaway from the SAAACA
1964	First mine cycle racing track was completed at the Vooruitzicht Mine
1964	Cycling activities at the Elkah Stadium in Rockville, Soweto
1970	SACF expelled from the International Cycling Union
1973	First Rapport Tour. Black riders George Pitso; Abie Oromeng; Sam Ramaboda; Jewboy Skelm Selatwe and Elias Ramantele participated clandestinely in Mozambique against a Portuguese team
1974	UWC Cycling Club established
1975	SA Championships at Esselen Park, Worcester
1979	Arthur (Archie) Barnwell of the Bayview Wheelers in Natal became the first non-white cycling Springbok
1982	Peter Nicholson becomes the first Coloured cyclist in the Rapport Tour
1978	SA Cycling Association joined the SA Cycling Federation under the banner of multi-racial sport
1978	SA Cycling Board established with affiliation to SACOS under the Presidency of Ivan Williams. Boland, Western Province and Eastern Province as founding members. Karoo joined later as 4th affiliate
1978	Boland Cycling Board established with Worcester Wheelers, Worcester Cycling Club; Thunderbird and Ceres as founding Clubs
1979	Swartklip Road Race hosted by Western Province
1980	Bloch Cycling Event, Esselen Park, Worcester, hosted by Boland Cycling Board
1981	Boland organizes Schus Datsun Tour de Boland under banner of SACB. Also, the first non-racial cycling league completion for schools in the Boland – Fariedas curtain Boland school cycling league
1984	SACB participate in SACOS Sports Festival
1989	SACB disband, resulting in no unity talks
1992	South Africa returns to the Olympic Movement

Source: Hendrik Snyders and Charles Beukes

115

WALL OF MEMORY

SA CYCLING ASSOCIATION [SACA] OFFICIALS PRE 1977

Cupido Green (Sr.)	'Father' of cycling in the Boland
Japie Green	SACA President
Essop Ismail	SACA Treasurer
Nick de Beer	SACA executive member
Peter Pieterse	SACA President
Edgar Rhoda	Griqualand West
Auburn Goliath	Eastern Province
A Hector	Eastern Province
Amelia Gerwel	Eastern Province
Anvis Karriem	Boland
John Africa	Boland
W Cloete (Sr)	SACA
Thomas Abrahams	Natal
Arthur Jacobs	Boland
W Cloete (Jr)	WP
Patrick Goosen	Border
Sulaiman Valley	Boland
Koos Philander	Boland

SA CYCLING BOARD [SACB] OFFICIALS POST 1977

Charles Beukes	President
WF Cloete	Patron
Ivan Williams	President
Walter Kruger	Secretary
Willie Cloete	Treasurer
Delicia Hendricks	Boland
Juanita Beets	Boland
Vanessa Williams	Western Province
Ihron Rensburg	Presidency
William Newman	Western Province
Dick Hendricks	Boland
Pikkie Crotz	Boland
Esme Hartogh	Boland
EC January	Secretary

References

Arendse, I. 2012. *Onse mense*. Cape Town: National Heritage Council.

Brink, T. 2017. *Cape Town Cycle Tour: The authorized history of the world's greatest bike race*. Maitland: Mapstudio.

Camplin, J. 2012. *The World's Greatest Cycle Tour: The story of the Cape Argus Pick 'n Pay Cycle Tour*. Cape Town: Kari Evans-Webb and Richard Webb.

Cleophas, F.J. 2014. A historical-social overview of athletics in 19th century Cape Colony, South Africa. *AJPHERD*, June, 20(2:1):585-592.

Coetzer, P. 1984. *Awaiting Trial: Allan Hendrickse*. Alberton: Librarius Felicitas.

Human, E. 1984. *Die Paarl se Boxing Day Sports*. Cape Town: San Publishers.

Jowett, W. 1981. *Centenary: 100 years of organised South African cycle racing*. South Africa: South African Cycling Federation.

Manenzhe, J. 2007. The politicisation of funerals in South Africa during the 20th century (1900-1994). Unpublished MA mini-thesis. Pretoria: University of Pretoria.

Ndlovu, M. 2013. "Mobilising History for nation-building in South Africa: A decolonial perspective." *Yesterday & Today*, 9:1–12, July.

O' Toole, S. 2013. "Apartheid was the spoke in South African cycling." *Mail & Guardian*, 8 March.

Wills, M. 2008. *The Cycle Tour*. Cape Town: Double Storey.

Sport historical significant moments in my life

Andrew September
Former South African Amateur Athletics Board athlete

In identifying historical significant moments in my sport life story, I am naturally coerced into relating a narrative that is entwined with the social, educational and political developments of Cape Town, South Africa. My school sport career started with an exposure to sport and physical education at Lourier Primary School[1] from 1971 to 1975 in the epicentre of a council development in the southern suburbs of Cape Town in Retreat. My story continues with high school sport experiences (athletics, gymnastics, volleyball) at Heathfield High School[2] that were accompanied by an awareness of political issues.[3] It continues with experiences in athletics and volleyball, first at the Hewat College[4] from 1981 to 1985 and finally the University of the Western Cape[5] from 1986 till 1988. After this, I entered the teaching profession where I taught physical education at various schools in the southern suburbs of Cape Town. In between, there are experiences that require reflection. After 1994, I represented Western Province in volleyball and gymnastics. I have also represented the post-apartheid South African athletics union, Athletics South Africa (ASA), in athletics.

In identifying historical significant moments in a Black Capetonian's sport life story, the narrator will be naturally coerced into relating a narrative that is entwined with educational and political developments of South Africa. This is also true of me. I was one of the founder members of the Skeletons Roller Skating Club from 1981 to 1985, a community-based club for mainly materially poor young people from my neighbourhood. I then enrolled at the University of the Western Cape to complete a degree in Human Movement Studies.[6] In between, there are experiences that warrant reflection. I had a coaching career in athletics

---

1   A public primary school, established in 1966, that grew out of the Dutch Reformed Mission School, Blouvlei. Lourier was administered by the Department of Coloured Affairs.
2   A public high school in the southern suburbs of Cape Town established in 1961 and administered by the Department of Coloured Affairs.
3   The school boycotts of 1980 and 1985 are emphasised by many Cape Town school teachers as the key years that combined schools and the struggle against apartheid. See Wieder A. 2003. *Voices from Cape Town Classrooms*, p. 71.
4   A teachers' training college in Crawford, Cape Town, named after a Cape School Board member, Ben Hewat, and opened in 1941.
5   Opened in 1959 as a University College for Coloured students in Bellville, Cape Town. Thomas, C., 2010. *Finding freedom in the bush of books. The UWC experience and spirit*, p. ix.
6   The Department of Physical Education started in 1983 and the first graduates graduated in 1985. Andrew September graduated in 1987.

and gymnastics prior to 1994. After 1994, I represented my province, Western Province, in volleyball and gymnastics and I also represented Athletics South Africa (ASA).

My sport career started in 1971 at Lourier Primary School and is still ongoing in 2017. People cannot believe that I am still an athlete. I reflect on people like Mr Andrew October[7] and Mr Winston Kloppers[8] who were instrumental in my development in terms of being a physical educator. It was because of those physical education teachers that we had a good education and understood our roles better as physical education teachers. We had a good approach to teaching.

When I was in Sub A or Sub B, I remember Mr John Small, Adam Small, the poet's dad, was the principal of this particular school. John Sylvester Small was principal at Lourier Primary School from 1966 till 1971. From 1945 till 1965, he was principal of the Blouvlei Dutch Reformed Mission School in Retreat where Mr October taught for a short while. Mr October told a friend of mine how difficult it was to teach at Blouvlei School because of the sand blowing in your face all the time. That Mr Small was also my mother's principal at Blouvlei Dutch Reformed School.

So here I am, writing about Lourier Primary School. That specific school had a good base for physical education, culture and academics. I can remember that in primary school years they had a themed concert, "The Water Year", which is especially good in Cape Town, since we are experiencing the worst drought in living memory. We had very good educators and teachers. Physical education skills were taught at an early age in Sub B and because of dedicated teachers, we received instruction in athletics, sprinting and jumping. In physical education we were taught gymnastics. Mr Richard Anthony, the physical educator, played a big role in our physical development during grades 5 and 7 (standard 3 to 5). He qualified as a physical education specialist in 1948 at the Wesley Training School (Cleophas, 2009:292). I was taught hurdles at Lourier. In grade 4 and grade 5 I was taught the Fosbury Flop, by Mr Adams at Steenberg Primary School. With limited resources these educators tried their best. We've realised many school achievements despite challenges.

At Heathfield High School there was a culture of sport. A vast amount of opportunities were available at school because of this. High jump and long jump, being two of my events that created such opportunities of achievement and growth. When I did the long jump, I would say, "I am sorry, you will have to make the pit longer." My personal best long jump distance was 7.20m, in grade 10 whilst my high jump height was 1.90 metres. When I was in grade 12, I jumped 2 metres. In triple jump I jumped 14 metres. Mr October was our physical educator and he taught us gymnastics. I participated in artistic gymnastics and successfully achieved Western Province colours. Mr Ismail Collier[9] was one of our coaches from grade 10 to grade 12. He played a pivotal role in the coaching of athletics. Many top athletes achieved great success as a result of his unselfish coaching commitment.

We also had many financial challenges. Essentials such as running attire were at the bottom of the priority list. We had no spikes. We shared a lot of travelling costs. Upon selection for

---

7   Andreas Hermanus October, born 31 January 1931. He qualified as a physical education specialist from the Wesley Training School in 1954, Cleophas FJ. 2009. Physical education in the Coloured community, p. 297.

8   Winston Kloppers, a physical education teacher and later lecturer at the University of the Western Cape. Kloppers was a qualified coach under a British Amateur Athletic Board scheme, see Cleophas, FJ. 2017. Creating a sport historian's life story.

9   Collier was originally from Natal whom he represented at national level in athletics.

the Province team, practices would take place mostly at Vygieskraal Stadium.[10] The first and second place winners in track events and first place winners in the high jump at the champion of champions meeting were considered for the Western Province team. The long jump participants were usually drawn from the sprinting team.

Freddie Williams[11] and I would walk or jump train[12] to the training field. When we reached Crawford station, we ran 3 kilometres to Vygieskraal Station. That was our warm-up. Going home was the same. It was unbelievable the standard we set. We trained thrice a day, every day, and the whole year. Before school from seven to a quarter to eight, after school with the school team, then five to six pm with the club team. From 1978 to 1980, I was part of the Western Province Senior Schools Union team (see Cleophas & Van der Merwe, F.J.G. 2009:701–713). Again, in those specific events, high jump, long jump, triple jump and sprinting. The team captains were Freddie Williams and Ingrid Miller (née Arendse). She was the first Coloured female student to graduate from the Physical Education department at Stellenbosch University.

At Athlone stadium, I jumped heights of 1.95 metres to 2.10 on a grass surface. People could not believe it because my height is only 1.75 metres. Our performances were not influenced by our poor facilities and lack of resources as a result of the country's politics. We still competed at a very high level.

I joined the South Peninsula Athletic Club[13] when I was in grade 8 in 1976. I can remember many times I saw how Terence Smith practised. In 1978 I achieved provincial colours for high jump and long jump. Of course, as I said earlier, there were many challenges: no specialised running spikes and of course the financial constraints. We often said, *"Can I borrow your spikes? I am going to jump now."* We still set high standards in those events – high jump, long jump, triple jump, sprinting and hurdles.

During 1976 to 1980 we participated under the South African Council on Sport (SACOS) banner, despite being prepared for international participation. I can remember when we were in grades 11 and 12, we realised we could not progress in South Africa but we wanted to compete internationally, in the Olympics. We could not achieve this officially through the South African Amateur Athletics (SAAAU)[14] competitions because SACOS had adopted a Double Standards Resolution (DSR).[15] The SAAAU was the government-sanctioned athletics body that operated within the apartheid system. With its establishment in 1894, it supported racial segregation and later it had separate racially defined controlling bodies. This was

---

10   This was a tartan track in the suburb of Athlone in Cape Town. It was used from 1981 by the Western Province Amateur Athletics and Cycling Association.
11   Freddie Williams obtained Springbok colours in 1982 and 1983. He represented Canada in the 800m in the 1992 Olympic Games.
12   A colloquial term for taking a train ride without paying for a ticket.
13   An athletic club that was started in the southern suburbs of Cape Town by, amongst others, Terence Smith.
14   The South African Amateur Athletic Association held it's first athletic meeting on 24 March 1894, Le Roux G. (Ed.). *90 Golden years*, p. 8. It dissolved in the 1990s as the South African Amateur Athletic Union (SAAAU) when Athletics South Africa was established. The last SAAAU president, Charles Niewoudt, was a member of the secret Afrikaner organisation, the Afrikaner Broederbond. See Strydom H & Wilkins I. 1978. *The Super Afrikaners*, p. A79.
15   The Double Standards Resolution (DSR) was a series of statements by the South African Council on Sport that determined the degree of contact between sportspersons and instruments of the apartheid regime.

unacceptable for us in SACOS. We, the South African Amateur Athletic Board, a SACOS affiliate, demanded a complete non-racial set-up in a non-racial society.

After grade 12 I applied to Hewat College in 1981 and studied there until 1985. There I extended my sport career, specifically studying physical education. I remember the hurdles events and the 100m final against Nazeem Smith. He held the SAAAB 100 metre record in a time of 10.2 seconds (Facebook, Athletics Clipboard).

During this period, I was a member of the Western Province College team and I got my national colours. I can remember Wilfie Daniels being our team manager at SAAAB competitions. He was from Cloetesville in Stellenbosch and helped establish the Stellenbosch Amateur Athletics Club in September 1976 (Facebook, Athletics clipboard). My personal best performances at club level were: high jump – 2.15m, long jump – 7.30m, triple jump – 14.80m and the 110 metre hurdles – 14.1 seconds. I was selected for the SAAB team during 1981 and 1990.

During this time, I was a founder member with a group that established the Skeletons Rollerskating Club. I was chairman and coach of the club. This was a great opportunity to get children off the streets and coach them in rollerskating. This club grew quickly to approximately 60 members. Our practice grounds were in the park in Allenby Drive[16] in the Retreat neighbourhood. Neighbours such as Mr and Mrs Bessick opened their hearts and doors to accommodate speakers, use of electricity, toilets and allowed meetings to take place in their garage. We appreciate such parents' support.

Completing my teaching diploma at Hewat, my aim was to continue my sport career as an athlete and physical educator. I initially applied to Stellenbosch University to study physical education. Initially my application was successful and I was called for an interview. There were questions, such as "Why do you want to study at our university and not at your university?" "If we accept you into the Maties team, what will SACOS do?" I said, "I am here to study." The professor also said, "Seeing as your other major is history, what is your perception on South Africa's next president?" I said, "If you remember the French Revolution, change is imminent. The people will change. I am sure a black president will be elected." After that, I was denied access to Stellenbosch University. I was accepted at the University of the Western Cape (UWC) in 1986 and then I became a member of athletic club there. I also received national colours that year when a SAAB team was selected after the South African championships in Durban. I remember Mr Colin Anders. He was a walker who completed the London to Brighton marathon walk in 1970 (*Cape Herald*, 1970:14). I took part in high jump, long jump, triple jump and 110 metre hurdles.

I received my club colours, provincial colours, and national colours. There was a competition between me and a Boland athlete, Daniel Orange. After beating Daniel Orange he asked me, "How is it possible that you are shorter than me and you can beat me?" I was jumping 2.14 to 2.15 metres. I said, "Surprises come in small packages."

After studying, I started my teaching career as a physical education teacher. I started at Grassdale High School.[17] Many years later, learners can still participate in sports like chess and badminton at this school. I coached many hours of sport after school, because of me

---

16 Named after Field Marshal Edmund Henry Hynman Allenby.
17 Established in 1983 in Grassy Park, Cape Town, as a working-class school.

trying to create opportunities for learners especially from disadvantaged communities. I remember where I came from. I started getting involved in coaching clinics. One was held in George. Another one I participated in was the IAAF Coaching Course. I served as part of the coaching structure for certain athletes that went up to world championships. An athlete who participated internationally was Simeon Marsh from Lavender Hill[18] who excelled in long jump and triple jump and as a result was chosen as part of the South African team that competed in Cuba, Hungary and Canada. On 7 November 1992 I got married to Melvina Williams and we have two sons, André and Dane. From an early age I coached my sons but it was André who took to athletics. He achieved national colours as a decathlon athlete during his high school years but he became specialised once he started studying Physiotherapy at University of Western Cape. He became one of the top hurdlers in varsity and club athletics.

After the age of 35 I started taking part in veteran athletics, specifically in high jump, long jump, triple jump and 110 m hurdles. I received many gold and silver medals. I received my WP and SA colours during this time again. It was during this time that I was selected to participate in Mauritius during the African Championships and the Namibian Championships and received gold in all my events.

References

Cape Herald, 12 September 1970.

Cleophas, F.J. 2009. Physical education and physical culture in the Coloured community of the Western Cape, 1837–1966. Unpublished PhD dissertation. Stellenbosch: Stellenbosch University.

Cleophas, F.J. & Van der Merwe, F.J.G. 2009. A historical overview of the Western Province Senior Schools Sports Union. 1956 to 1973. *African Journal for Physical, Health Education, Recreation and Dance (AJPHERD),*15(4), December 2009:701–713.

Cleophas, F.J. 2017. Creating a sport historian's life story narrative in society. *The International Journal of the History of Sport.* https://doi.org//10.1080/09523367.2017.1383386

Facebook. Athletics clipboard.

Le Roux, G. (ed.). *90 Golden years*. Pretoria: SAAAU.

New World Foundation. 2017. *Women Surviving Lavender Hill.* Lavender Hill: New World Foundation.

Southern Mail. 2011. 16 March.

Strydom, H. & Wilkins, I. 1978. *The Super Afrikaners: Inside the Afrikaner Broederbond.* Johannesburg: Jonathan Ball.

Thomas, C. 2010. *Finding freedom in the bush of books. The UWC experience and spirit.* Selbourne: Wendy's Book Lounge.

Wieder, A. 2003. *Voices from Cape Town classrooms. Oral histories of teachers who fought Apartheid.* Bellville: University of the Western Cape.

---

18 A sub-economic township on the Cape Flats that was built for evictees from Lavender Hill, District Six. In 2011, residents were living in fear for their lives due to gang violence, *Southern Mail,* 2011. 16 March, pp. 1, 4. For daily life experience see New World Foundation, 2017. *Women Surviving Lavender Hill.*

Andrew September, provincial hurdler under the SACOS banner
Source: Andrew September

Andrew September (far left) against Nazeem Smith in front in 100m at College championship in 1985
Source: Andrew September

Skeletons Rollerskating Club
Source: Andrew September

Skeletons Rollerskating Club
Source: Andrew September

Skeletons Rollerskating Club – Juniors
Source: Andrew September

Colin Anders standing front left next to Andrew September as part of the
Western Province team in 1986
Source: Andrew September

Human Movement Studies final-year class in 1987. Andrew September is standing 7th from left in back row. Source: Francois Cleophas

André September, son of Andrew September
Source: Andrew September

Andrew September, third from right in front, at IAAF coaching clinic
Source: Andrew September

Andrew September, veteran athlete
Source: Andrew September

Andrew September, veteran athlete, African Athletics Championships, Mauritius. Source: Andrew September

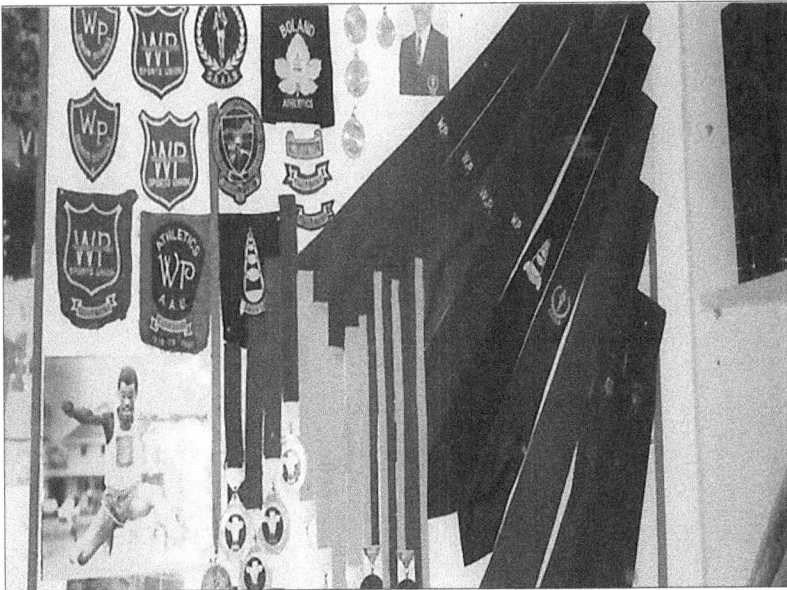

Andrew September's partial archive
Source: Andrew September

My changing and continual life story in non-racial sport

André Alexander

Former SACOS baseball player; South African Soccer Federation player and national school athletics champion

I hail from a Cape Town suburb in Crawford called Rutvale Estate. I come from a big family of eight, with my parents making up the ten, and all of us participated in sport. All the Alexanders come from Silvertown and Bonteheuwel[1] townships and they were footballers. My sisters were involved in hockey and netball and in terms of my claim to fame, I was introduced to Spartans Athletics Club by my sister Sharon. She was also a legend as an Oaklands High School sprinter. I came to Spartans Amateur Athletic Club and Robin April and Herman Abrahams were the administrators. It was discipline. If you did not come to the Thursday training, you could not participate on the Saturday. So I never came to Tuesday training, I only came to Thursday training and made sure I made the team. I am going to share a little bit about my continual life story in non-racial sport and it is really just my story.

My dad, David Abraham Alexander, was a provincial table tennis player[2] and footballer with his brothers for the Ridgeville Football Club.[3] My first experience of primary school athletics was when I attended Thornton Road Primary School.[4] I think of those other athletes whom I ran against, I do not think they are in athletics or the coaching realm today.

I have heard many people in non-racial sport talk about other people influencing your life. I had a Hewat trained[5] physical education teacher, Yvonne Kleintjies, that was actually

---

[1] A *Cape Herald* reporter described Bonteheuwel in 1973 as a place where "poverty and lack of public amenities are the two main ingredients in a concoction of crime and violence labelled 'social frustration' and usually found in South African townships", *Cape Herald*. 1973. 28 April, p. 13. Many whites were oblivious of life in Bonteheuwel. When a City Councillor, Tom Walters, described the poor living conditions of Bonteheuwel to a predominantly white audience in 1973, "some gasped and even laughed", *Cape Herald*, 1973. 20 October, p. 13.

[2] David Alexander played for the Stephanians Table Tennis Club that grew out of the Stephanians Football Club. The Stephanian Football Club was founded in 1924 in Loader Street, Green Point, by Pastor Andrews, and the Meyer and Groenewald families. It was named after a young man, with Philippine family connections, Stephen Hilario, from the Green Point area who drowned while swimming off the old pier. A netball club also grew out of the Stephanian Football Club in the 1950s.

[3] This was the Ridgeville Football Club.

[4] Thornton is situated in the southern suburbs of Cape Town, 10 kilometres east of the city centre, sitting close to the border delineating the Northern and Southern Suburbs.

[5] Hewat Teacher Training College (later known known as Hewat College) was established in 1941 and started training specialist male physical education teachers from 1961 and women from 1966. The College was

my mentor – my mother after school – she saw the potential I had inside, and walked the road with me from Standard One to Standard Five. I had the opportunity to develop as a young man. In 1978 I was at Turfhall Primary[6] and had a niggling hamstring injury. I never participated that year. I was devastated because athletics was the summer code and then obviously football was the winter code. That made it very disheartening for me. I was always a go-getter and wanted to achieve as much as I could. I attended the Spes Bona High School[7] and represented it at the Western Province Senior Schools Sports Union athletic meetings at the Athlone Stadium. A common thing amongst us was 'hand-me-downs'. That was my experience of primary school athletics. I remember running at the Gelvandale Stadium at Port Elizabeth on Ash Track and I had to borrow my sister, Sharon's, spikes that curled around my toes, and I ran with no starting blocks. The starting blocks I used were Sharon's, which were the old aluminum blocks with a little pipe that you use to keep your starting blocks in place. I got my coaching through the Spartans Athletics Club, as well as by the late Mr Ishmael Collier, who had a huge influence on my work ethic. I used to get up at six in the morning, walk down to Crawford in Repulse Road and down to Clover Crescent.[8] At seven thirty we had to start walking back to Spes Bona. I always missed the double period on a Monday for mathematics class. I failed Mathematics in matric, by the way, and I had to redo that as a supplementary.

A friend, Caval Alexander, who was actually a star rugby player pushed me in terms of my athletics. He would be there at half past six as well, walk from Kewtown[9] and get to Clover Crescent and we would be training at six thirty in the morning and again in the afternoons. He would walk down to the Hewat College Ash Track and start working out with me. I realised that one of the other things in life is iron sharpens iron and that this young man kept me on the brink of making sure that I was pushing the boundaries, that I was achieving what we set out to do in terms of school athletics. He was always the one running second to me in our inter-schools.

I ran the 100 m in 10.6 seconds on grass at the Athlone Stadium in 1982. I had a start that day. My claim to fame is that Mr Ismail Collier used two big blocks that he clapped in my ear for reaction time. Then we would have the starting position and again he would smack in my ear; by the time I went home after about twenty starts, I was deaf in my right ear. Teachers often asked, 'Why are you not listening in class?'. My coach was to be blamed for that. In terms of my development, physically, I was undernourished. We had one or two meals, and we had to fight for the last two slices of bread with eight siblings. So, I grew up with a developmental disadvantage and I never used any weights. We did not have those sort of things around. I ran with only my body mass.

As a 13-year-old I had the privilege of seeing Edmund Lewis run. Poetry in motion is what I said to my wife. If ever I wanted to demonstrate the action of running, I would want to imitate Lewis to the 'T'. When he was in top gear you heard him go "Choop! Choop! Choop! Choop! Choop!" He had far bigger muscles and you knew if he was coming around the

---

6   Turfhall Primary was a public school opened in 1973 in Thornton Road, Crawford.

administered by the Department of Coloured Affairs, later known as House of Representatives.

7   A Cape Town high school that was administered by the Coloured Affairs Department. The WPSSSSU held its quarterly and annual general meetings at this venue.

8   Clover Crescent was adjacent to Athlone Stadium and was used by hockey clubs and schools as training fields.

9   Q-town (later Kew Town) in Athlone, Cape Town, is a Second World War sub-economic housing development scheme for the Coloured population of the inner city areas.

two-hundred-metre bend and somebody was ahead of him they only knew it was Edmund Lewis 'The Train' coming past and people would just say: "Wow, the race is over, Edmund's winning this." I had the privilege of leading the WPSSSU team in 1982 with Dianne Carelse (now Morgan). This was an opportunity of being able to have the moment of leading without understanding that leadership was developing in me. Someone saw the potential in me to be able to lead a team of one hundred athletes onto Athlone Stadium and then thank – we were the host that year – the other provinces which was probably five hundred athletes at the Spes Bona Hall that particular evening at the prize giving. For me that was overwhelming, but it gave me an opportunity to realise that: *You know what, André, you are a boy from Crawford that speaks a bit of English and a whole lot of Afrikaans, with the other words in between, but you have some leadership in you, and you make life what it is through your circumstances and your experiences.* This was one of the experiences I believe that gave me the stepping-stone to be able to continue being involved in sport.

After my final race in high school, I never went on to run in another event. I remember that 10.6 seconds in the 100 metres, beating Nazeem Moos. Clement du Plessis kept asking me, *"Why don't you continue with club athletics?"* Well, it is because my wife, Amanda Alexander, and I met on a baseball field and that changed my life. Amanda and I met at fifteen, courted for fifteen years, we are married for thirty-one years. I have known her for 46 years. Together we are serving our local communities through baseball and softball and I do a bit of football coaching as well. She is still an administrator in softball, very much involved as a life member at the soccer club. She shaped the other part of me, because whenever I came off the track and proudly told Clement du Plessis, *"Clement, did you see that race?"* she, Amanda, will come and say, *"André, you did not do very well today, in fact keep quiet because Cavel Marthinussen beat you."*

My wife and I had the privilege of being able to be the first couple to represent SACOS at the 1982 SACOS games as a couple. She was the catcher in the softball team; I was in the baseball team. There were 2,000 people at the UWC stadium coming to watch baseball, while there was another event taking place at Athlone Stadium, that particular Friday or Saturday evening. That was my moment of glory in terms of understanding what it means to represent your country because in that particular team were players from Eastern Province and Johannesburg. Durban did not have baseball back then. We were then the fully representative team of South Africa and we were called Quaggas.

In football it was a scoutmaster, Bernie Kannemeyer, that stayed in Denchworth Avenue that had a huge impact in my life at the Blackheath Football Club.[10] After I won the 100 metres, a professional football manager said, *we need this winger to come and play for us.* I thus had the opportunity to play professional football. I played in the South African Professional Soccer Federation[11] at Athlone Stadium at the age of 17 alongside Duncan Crowie.[12] Boebie Solomons was our player/coach.[13]

---

10 An amateur soccer club, based in the suburb of Athlone that was affiliate to the SASF.
11 See Chapter, 'Discord in the dressing room'.
12 A retired South African football (soccer) striker who mostly played for the professional club Santos Cape Town in the SASF.
13 A professional football player for Glendene United and Cape Town Spurs clubs in Cape Town. He coached professional clubs in the 21st century and was also a national coach for the Under 20 team in 1998.

I need to honour my wife because she was part of this legacy of shaping and molding my personal life. So much so that that I serve five regions in the rural communities through the Department of Culture and Sport (DECAS) High Performance Academy's with eight disciplines in them, an average of thirty athletes, and we provide funding for gym work, for going to see the sport psychologist, going to see the physiotherapist and going to the doctor. I manage government funding and make sure it ends up with the child in Manenberg for example. The continuous impact that apartheid had on me, did not make me bitter but I was angry because I never had the chance to run against or play football against white counterparts. I do realise God had a greater purpose for me – to be able to serve our communities – and today to be able to share that story, which has been placed somewhere in my scrapbook.

André Alexander (left) and Caval Alexander (right)
Picture taken at Athlone Stadium with Kewtown housing
scheme in background. Source: André Alexander

ANDRE ALEXANDER (links) van die Westelike Provinsie, wat gister die 100 m in 10,7 sek. gewen het en net voor sy spanmaat, Nazeem Moos, oor die wenstreep was in die wedloop vir seuns o.17 in die SA Senior Skole-atletiekvereniging se byeenkoms wat in die Athlone-stadion gehou is. (Foto: Jack Lestrade.)

André Alexander (left) and Nazeem Moos (right) in the
South African Senior School's Association championship in 1982
100m final. Source: André Alexander

South African Council on Sport (SACOS) baseball team in 1982. André Alexander is crouching third from left. Source: André Alexander

André Alexander with Glendene
United professional soccer club
Source: André Alexander

GLENDENE UNITED wat alles sal uithaal om die gunsteling oo te stof. Die span is agter van links: Edgar Carolse (massour), Ralph Onstkruidt, Edwin Sauls, Philip Priem, mnr. Moegamat Zain Allie (bestuurder), Isaac Arepo, Mansoor Abdullah, Melvyn Sauls. Voor: Cyril Morrigan, Andre Alexander, Michael Smith, Bretto Solomons, Trevor Manuel, George van Niekerk en Duncan Crowie.
Foto's: SHARRIEF JAFFER

References

Cape Herald, The. 1973. 28 April.

Cape Herald, The. 1973. 20 October.

Cleophas F.J. & Van der Merwe F.J.G. 2009. A historical overview of the Western Province Senior Schools Sports Union, 1956 to 1973. *African Journal for Physical, Health Education, Recreation and Dance*, 15(4):701–713.

Sprinting with controversy

Shaun Vester
Former SAAAB athletic champion

My sport life story is characterised by success, injury and disappointment. I entered non-racial athletics as a 15-year-old sprinter for Grassy Park Athletic Club in 1985. I ran 10,5 seconds in the 100 metres that year at the South African Athletics Amateur Athletic Board (SAAAB) Prestige meeting that year at Vygieskraal. The following year I ran a time of 10,4 seconds at the University of the Western Cape Stadium at the SACOS festival. My time was 10,4 seconds in 1987 at Vygieksraal Stadium at the SAAB Prestige Meeting. Then my career ended in 1988 with a personal best time of 10,1 seconds under controversial circumstances. At the end of that year I ran a personal best time of 20,8 seconds in the 200 metres, under similar controversial circumstances. On reflection, my short career, filled with injuries and other controversies, is similar to most of my predecessors whose sport life remains off the radar of historical interest.

It is an honour to share my historical athletic moments with the public and just to help talk and write about what we achieved in non-racial sport in South Africa. My athletic career started with a vision and that was to become world champion in a 100m race, to do my best, to give my best in sport and also to compete internationally. I started in the days of the Apartheid regime where I endured many trying circumstances and faced many challenges. My athletics life story started in 1984 and ended in 1990.

I do not have much evidence of my primary school events but I can remember the days when I had to borrow spikes and run without starting blocks because of the financial situation I faced at home. My first recorded time was 10.9 seconds. I did not know anything about times, I just ran.

I graduated to high school where I started performing at club level. I joined the Grassy Park Athletics Club in 1985 after Christelle Jansen approached me, and signed me up after she saw my performances. She instilled the vision in my heart to become world champion in the years to come. I believed that I could become a world champion and I practised very hard. In 1985 at the South African Senior Schools' Sports Association (SASSSA) and the South African Amateur Athletics Board (SAAAB) Prestige Meeting at the Vygieskraal Stadium I clocked a time of 10.5 seconds, unaware that I equalled the senior men's 100m record. This was done without state-of-the-art infrastructure and facilities.

I ran a string of 10.5's, 10.4's and 10.3's. Due to that, in 1986, guys like Clement du Plessis, Wilfred Daniels and Andrew September approached me and told me: "Your talent is obvious and you must be coached." I used the facilities of the University of the Western Cape (UWC) Stadium where Mr Wilfie Daniels mentored and coached us. I ran a 10.2 seconds, once again without starting blocks and with borrowed spikes. I was just hoping to get the proper size for me competing in that race. I was not aware I was in the race until Cedric van Wyk told me *"Meneer what are you doing on the sideline?"* (Mister, what are you doing on the sideline?). I had to take my jeans off, my top, my jacket, whatever I had on. I had to phone mom to get to the stadium on time. So I went to the men's 100m sprinter Nazeem Smith, and he gave me one of his athletes' spikes, there were still spikes out. One of my highlights was when the watches stopped at 9.9 seconds as a nineteen-year-old with borrowed spikes from Nazeem Smith. There was a controversy regarding my time. I was quite surprised I got that time and later that season, Johan Rossouw, running in the South African Amateur Athletics Union (SAAAU) clocked a time of 10.1 seconds. Johan Rossouw was an awesome 100m sprinter. After I had finished my sport career, I spoke to him and I shook his hand and we discussed times and performances.

I was beaten by Craig Steyn from Stellenbosch. He actually became the Speed Merchant and I highly respected him. I was nicknamed the Blue Train and I think Nazeem Smith wanted that name but it was given to me. I asked Nazeem, "How did you get it right to run a 21.4 at Dal Jasofat Stadium?" He said to me, "I will teach you how to run." So, I had a good understanding and relationship with my fellow athletes that I competed against. I actually learned from them how to become a better athlete. They told me: "I do not want to beat you, I want to beat your time."

I got my pre-season work done on the dunes while my friends where swimming. Then I came close to 20.6 at the end of the season in 1988. Because of my performance in the 100m I was rewarded with a sponsorship from *Reader's Digest* in 1988 whereby the funds were given to me for education use, for extra tutoring in classes, and the opportunity to have my own spikes. Sadly, my career was cut short in 1988 when I was plagued by a severe hamstring injury. I made many comebacks at that time. But my plans for competing nationally and overseas never materialised.

I had a good time in the communities, helping athletes in disadvantaged areas and imparting my knowledge and experience of sprinting events. My aim was to take people to a level I have never been and to take them overseas where I have never been. Today still, I feel like being number one, it never departed from me, that dream, that passion, I still have that dream at 50. It was an honour to follow in the footsteps of Terence Smith and a lot of other guys. To Wilfred Daniels, I always salute you for the space you have given me to do my preparation. It has been an honour to be part of non-racial sport for many years.

Shaun Vester in winning action. Source: Facebook: Athletics clipboard

A history of South African cross-country, middle- and long-distance running and walking

Dewald Steyn
Athletic historian

Maybe I must first give my background, explaining why I wrote a book (Steyn, 2015) and why I am writing a second book, "Total Track and Field History of South African Athletics". At school I was a hurdler but I played rugby which was more important to me. In my third year at Potchefstroom University for Christian Higher Education (commonly known as Potch)[1] I was the first team scrumhalf. I was secretary of the rugby club and I was always involved in organising. On 1 April 1964, that was before the Olympic Games that year, Peter Snell, the New Zeeland Olympic 800m gold medalist in 1960 and 800 metre and 1500 metre champion and his famous coach, Arthur Lydiard, gave a talk in Potchefstroom. Incidentally, Snell was also the 800 metre world record holder and first person to run a sub 4-minute mile in Africa in 1964. The next day I took my books back to rugby and said, "I am not playing rugby any more. I am an athlete now". So I became a long-distance athlete.

I knew I had some talent because early on that year I beat all the provincial runners, while I was a rugby player, in a cross-country race. I became deeply involved in organising and managing athletes and organising matches and all that, and represented five different provinces through the years. I competed in 72 South African championships in track, cross-country and road running and ran the Comrades Marathon, an annual 90 km road race between Durban and Pietermaritzburg in the Province of KwaZulu-Natal, winning the Hardy Ballington trophy, awarded to the best novice in 1975.

Then I started getting involved with black athletes. One Sunday, someone knocked on my back door, and there was a young athlete by the name of Hendrik Maako who got a bursary to go and study in the USA. If you got a bursary, that was it, you do not pay anything once you are there, but you have to get there on your own. He unsuccessfully tried for three months to find a sponsor to buy a ticket. I got him onto a plane on the Tuesday. He studied, finished and came home but today he is back in America. When he came back, after a short while, he said he was tired of looking over his shoulder not feeling safe, and went back to America. I also got involved with clubs and organising black athletes, and got the Reggie Walker Award from Athletics South Africa (ASA) in 1992 for special services I had rendered to athletics in South Africa. So, that is my background.

---

[1] Opening on 29 November 1869, in the capital of the former Zuid Afrikaanse Republiek, this university was established on firm Calvinist principles, an integral part of Afrikaner identity, *Mail & Guardian*, 2016, 4 March.

Now for me the history is about the athletes. Without the athlete there is no sport, so the athlete becomes number one. I do not so much care about the coaches, although I know there is no athlete without a coach, there is no athlete without organising, but you can be the best organiser you are, and if there are no athletes there is nothing. In my book, or books, it is more about athletes than anything else, but the way to find information, that is the big problem. Luckily I got hold of a lot of very good information. The Springbok miler of 1923, Will Vogt, was the secretary of the South African Amateur Athletic Union (SAAAU) for many years. In 1952 he published a book on the history of all the different provinces, the winners and the champions, and since 1952 Allister Mathews, Harry Beinart and Arrie Joubert yearly published an annual statistics book with all the information. I also got hold of the original results of the SAAAU since 1894 up to 1992. Also, the minutes of the SAAAU. Other information I got from Douglas Coghlan's PhD, 'The Development of Athletics in South Africa 1814 to 1914'. You would not realise that actually the British brought athletics to South Africa, especially KwaZulu-Natal, fighting the Zulus, and they had athletes, top athletes in the army, so they competed a lot. I also worked through *Honderd Jaar Matie Atletiek*, (Van der Merwe 1984)[2] and then also *WITS sport, and history of sport at the University of the Witwatersrand* (Winch 1989). There is a lot of information available there.

I found out that as far back as 1863 there was a black athlete with the name Simeon, who came second place behind W. Day in the 880 yards in Cape Town at the marriage celebrations of the Prince of Wales.[3] There was a guy by the name of Makwena who won the mile in 4 minutes 53 seconds. The SAAAU was established on 24 March 1894 as the South African Amateur Athletics Association, providing athletics and cycling participation.[4]

There is a whole list of black athletes who competed before 1894 and it was interesting to see that in the Eastern Province they had events for black athletes and at every event they were competing. Sometimes they were competing against whites and sometimes they had their own races. After the Second South African War this disappeared,[5] there was no more racist-free sport for blacks. There were few exceptions to this – one being the Ciskei Bantu Amateur Athletic Association (CBAAA) that had participation across the Colour Bar. On 1 October 1921, Transvaal University College (University of Pretoria), Johannesburg University College (University of the Witwatersrand) and Grey University College (University of the Free State) inaugurated the Dalrymple Cup Competition under the direction of Pete Suzman and Jan Hendrik Hofmeyer, the Johannesburg University College principal. Suzman and Hofmeyer were motivated by the South African Party's Conciliation policy at the time.[6] This policy was based on a desire that English and Afrikaans whites "would live together ... in one nation".[7] The black colleges were therefore excluded from this competition.

What was interesting is that from 1923 to at least 1957 black colleges in the Eastern Cape – Fort Hare University College, Lovedale College, Healdtown College, St. Matthews College,

2 A 186 page semi-glossy publication on the centenary history of the Stellenbosch University Athletic Club, Written in the Von Ranke style, it is filled with achievements of athletes, ignoring political and social dilemmas of the day.

3 *Cape Argus, The*. 1863. Marriage festival supplement. 21 May, p. 1.

4 The SAAAU mutated into Athletics South Africa (ASA) in 1996.

5 This was the war between Britain and the two Boer republics, the Zuid Afrikaanse Republiek and the Oranje Vrystaat with blacks on both sides. After the war, the peace treaty of Vereeniging disenfranchised blacks in the northern colonies and increasing racist legislation was passed against them.

6 Joubert A. 1985. *The history of Inter-Varsity Sport in South Africa*, Foreword, p. 8.

7 Kallaway P. 1987. *History alive*. p. 435.

Fort Cox College and St Matthews College – had a yearly competition. I have the results for the 1946 and 1947 meetings and in 1946 there was an athletics meeting between Fort Hare and Rhodes University. In that meeting there was a Springbok long jumper, Dennis Hasenjager, who finished second in the 100 yards and the 220 yards. He represented South Africa in long jump against a touring team of the USA in 1950. There is a story that the first meeting of a black runner running against whites in Africa was a guy by the name of Jonathan Malaya, who beat Gordon Pirie, a British Olympian, in 1958 in what used to be Salisbury, now Harare. This story is therefore not true, because the athletics meeting between the Universities of Rhodes and Fort Hare was actually the first one. Fort Hare had famous people who were top athletes. Sir Seretsi Khama of Botswana was a well-known shot-putter, while Robert Mugabe was apparently a good 440 yards runner. Then there was also Ysuf Lule who attended Fort Hare between 1936 and 1939 and succeeded Idi Amin in Uganda, who was also an 880 yards runner and once the National Champion in Uganda. T. Soobiah, a Natal Indian with a high ranking in the British Army, was a dominant sprinter.

The first black South African athletes to run in the Olympic Games were two Tswana farm workers, Jan Mashiane and Len Tau, from General Piet Cronje's farm. Cronje was a general in the Anglo-Boer War, who surrendered to the British during the war and participated in a review that re-enacted South African War scenes in Fillis Circis in St. Louis in 1904 (Loots, 2011). In 1904 the Olympics was in St. Louis in America and they moved it from Washington to St. Louis because the World Fair was there and the Americans said anyone could compete in the Olympics, so Mashiane and Tau ran in the marathon, and they actually finished 9th and 12th. There are stories that they were chased by a dog. The one story is that one was chased, and another story said that both were chased. There was a small write-up in an American paper saying *"Zulu Warrior Chased by Dog"* because they thought all blacks were Zulus. I once picked up in one of the statistics books that they gave Len Tau Springbok colours, which is not true. Somebody decided that because he ran in the Olympics, being South African, he must be a Springbok, but there were no Springboks in 1904.

My big problem these days is actually to find further information. Where my first book, a five-volume collection, was called *South African History of Cross Country Middle and Long Distance Running and Walking*, I decided to compile the total track history which might be double that thick. In the first book, I got some information about South African Amateur Athletic Board (SAAAB) athletes. I was able to get information from Jantjie Marthinus, ex SAAAB athlete who later became a SAAAU athlete; Johan Landsman, ex SAAAB athlete who later became a SAAAU athlete; and Wilfred Daniels, an ex-SAAAB athlete. The biggest problem is that I have been struggling to find information from ex athletes.

I have been working through the National Library of South Africa to find the origin of SAAAB and I could only find one academic work on the origin of the South African Amateur Athletic Board (Cleophas 2013). I did also find an article about a meeting on the 5th of February 1946 deciding to start this South Africa Amateur Athletics Board, but nobody can tell me where to get the original results. I found a newspaper that said the first Championships meeting was held on the 1st and 2nd of January 1948 in Paarl. The second championship was held also in January in 1950 and that was in Durban. The third championship was only held in 1953. They did not have a meeting every year, while they also jumped between the months of January and April. I found a lot of information in the *Sun* newspaper, which however closed in 1956. The next newspaper I could find, that has information, was the *Cape Herald* that started in 1965. So there is a 10-year gap. For my first book I worked through the scrapbooks of 100 ex-athletes. What I really need is the information of the SAAAB athletes, the ex-athletes and their scrapbooks. I do not even have their birthdates.

References

Cleophas, F.J. 2013. Contexting an ad hoc athletics unity in Natal, 1945–48. *SAJRSPER*. 35(2):15–36.

Joubert, A. 1985. *The History of Inter-Varsity Sport in South Africa*, Looking back with Pete Suzman. Natal; Suid-Afrikaanse Universiteite Atletiekvereniging.

Kallaway, P. 1987. *History Alive. Standard 10*. Pietermaritzburg: Shuter & Shooter.

Loots, S. 2011. *Sirkusboere*. Cape Town: Tafelberg.

Le Roux, G. 1984. *90 Golden Years*. Pretoria: SAAU.

Mail & Guardian. 2016. 4 March.

Steyn, D. 2015. *History of South African Cross-Country, Middle- and Long-Distance Running and Walking – 1894 to 2014*. Pretoria: D. Steyn.

Van der Merwe, F.J.G. 1984. *Honderd jaar Matie atletiek, 1885–1985*. Stellenbosch: Stellenbosch Athletic Club.

Winch J. 1989. *Wits Sport: An Illustrated History of Sport at the University of the Witwatersrand, Johannesburg*. Emmarentia: Windsor.

Programme of inaugural SAAAB championships
Source: F. Cleophas, private collection

A non-racial athletic president's life story

Robin April
Former president of the Western Province Amateur Athletics and Cycling Association

Although we lived and worked in trying times, athletics gave me lots of joy and very good memories. The president is only as good as his co-workers are, especially those who worked with me. It is like being at a funeral: when they give the tribute you only hear the good things about that person. Maybe it is because the bad things will take too long to tell. Unfortunately, I am speaking only about the good things of this president's past.

I have lived in Cape Town for most of my life, more than fifty years. I was born in Paarl and I come from a sporting family. My father was a South African tennis champion from 1934 to 1942 – I speak under correction. I have some certificates and memorabilia of his. Although I come from a sporting family, I never hear anything about my father having been the champion.

I had a good sporting experience at primary school. I used to run in the sprints and when I got to high school, Noorder-Paarl High,[1] in standard six and seven I found out that I was not as fast as I thought I was. I had to run in the mile and I never got into the first ten or twenty athletes who were running that day. Then I went to Genadendal. My mother posted me to a boarding school because *ek was 'n bietjie van 'n stoute ou gewees* (I was a bit of a naughty boy). Genadendal[2] was a very academic school,[3] no sports in standard eight and nine, and when I got to matric we started playing rugby. That was actually my first love. I grew up in an area where rugby was the game. I played for Rangers.[4] I was actually fifteen or sixteen years old when I played in their first team as scrumhalf. I was close to six foot but played as scrumhalf. My sporting career really took off at Hewat Training College.[5] I played first team rugby and I played with many a great player but I am just going to mention Maurice Heemro. In my opinion he was the best centre I have ever seen. He could 'break' off any foot. I also ran

---

1   Noorder Paarl High School grew out of the Athlone Training School in Paarl that traces its origins to the Bethel Congregational School (established 1892), *Sun* 1935, p. 7; *Sun* 1939, p. 2.
2   The first mission station in South Africa, dating back to 1737 that developed a unique physical education programme during the last decade of the 19th century, based on the philosophy of Johann Comenius, during the late decade of the 19th century, Cleophas FJ. 2009. Physical education and physical culture in the Coloured community of the Western Cape, 1837–1966. Unpublished PhD dissertation. Stellenbosch: Stellenbosch University. 104–107.
3   Present-day Emil Weder High School that can trace its origins to the work of Bishop Hans Peter Hallbeck in Genadendal in 1827.
4   A rugby club in Paarl established in 1914.
5   Robin April attended Hewat College from 1964 till 1968.

in the inter-schools with great success and captained the Western Province Senior Schools team in 1968. There was not much choice for a career option in my day. You either had to go into the building industry, become a policeman or go into education. My mother thought I would become a priest. To her dismay, I did not.

Sport career

I became the South African 400m, 800m, and 1500m champion at senior level in SAAAB. I eventually stopped athletics as it was organised very poorly. We would go on training camps for a week or more, and then when we came back from camps, the events were cancelled.

I was selected for the City and Suburban Rugby Union team, a South African Rugby Union (SARU) affiliate[6]. All the people who played for SARU in the past were offered blazers by the current South African Rugby Union. I cannot tell you what I really said, but this was more or less my response, *"Tell the people that are in charge to take this blazer and shove it up ..."* How could I have accepted a Springbok blazer when I did not play for them? In any case, I would have said we were not eligible during the Apartheid years – why do we suddenly qualify now? Many of the players condoned this tokenism by accepting the blazers.

Sport administration

Athletics, as an individual sport, is one of the most difficult codes to administer and it involves lots of sacrifice and time. My career as an administrator began at Hewat College, where I was a founding member and the chairman of the rugby and athletics club.[7] I became notorious for my no-nonsense approach. While I was teaching, I became the athletics convener for the Athlone Primary Schools' Sports Union[8] under Vincent Farrel.[9] He was a very outspoken chap and he was banned to Sutherland and that was the end of him because they really treated him badly. I introduced new methods of organising and managing athletics and was fortunate to have had a group of dedicated administrators to work with. Officials' courses were introduced to train and equip officials to run smooth athletics meetings.

In 1971 I started the Spartans Athletics Club, affiliated to the Western Province Amateur Athletics and Cycling Association (WPAACA). At that time athletics and cycling organised events together. A year after that I became the sports secretary of the WPAACA under Syd

---

6   The SARU grew out of the South African Coloured Rugby Football Board, established in 1896 in Kimberley and the City and Suburban Rugby Football Union was established in 1898, Booley A. 1998. *Forgotten heroes*, pp. 13, 155.

7   Norman Stoffberg, the physical education lecturer, along with Robin April were the initiators of the athletics club in 1967. For background information on Stoffberg see Cleophas FJ. 2009. Physical education and physical culture in the Coloured community of the Western Cape, 1837–1966. Unpublished PhD dissertation. Stellenbosch: Stellenbosch University. 86. The Hewat Rugby Club affiliated to the City and Suburban Rugby Football Union in 1966, Kloppers W. 2018. Telephonic interview.

8   The Athlone Schools' Sports Union was established in 1939 and provided sport for schools in the Athlone area and adjacent districts. It provided rugby, tenniquoit, soccer, cricket and athletics codes for boys. Girls were provided with netball and tenniquoits. The first executive was E.F. Doman, (chairman), Miss Abercrombie (from St. Raphael's School, secretary) and Mr. Lenders (from Central School, treasurer), *Cape Standard*, 25 April 1939, p. 13; *Sun*, 28 April 1939, p. 9.

9   Farrell was an also executive official of the Western Province Cricket Board 1972 (*Cape Herald*, 16 September 1972, p. 18). His employer, the Coloured Affairs Department, banished him to an isolated rural village, Sutherland, for his outspokeness against state policy (Western Province Cricket Board, 1982, p. 3).

Lotter, who was elected president in 1970. He brought with him a rich experience in the world of sport. In 1950 his curriculum vitae included: vice-chairman of the Crofton Harriers Athletic Club (1923–1924); founder member of the Cape Peninsula Junior Football Association and secretary for many years; vice-president of the Mellville Cricket Club; president of the Ashley Rangers AFC; president of Hotspurs AFC (1938-1950); president and founder member of the Olympic Card Union; chairman of the Western Province Table Tennis Union since 1939; chairman of the Utopian Table Tennis Club; runner-up in the Western Province table tennis championship in 1950; president of the South African National Table Tennis Board; president of Perthshire Table Tennis Club; vice-president of Ashley Table Tennis Club; vice-president of Durban and District Table Tennis Union; ex-secretary of Western Province Football Board; vice-president of Alliance Football League; organising secretary of the 1950 mass soccer tournament held in Cape Town; founder member of the Cape Peninsula Lawn Tennis Association; founder member of Nil Desperandum Lawn Tennis Club; chairman of Walmer Tennis Club (1932–1940) and president of the Malverns Cricket Club (1952). He was also an active trade unionist.[10] When important sport functions for different sport codes were held, he was often invited to do the presentation.

I became president of the WPAACA during the 1976/77 season, working with many competent people – Herman Abrahams, Winston Kloppers,[11] Wilfred Daniels,[12] Willy Davis[13] and Cedric Van Wyk,[14] to name but a few. We set ourselves high goals to improve the standard of athletics in the Western Province. Wilfred was the only track coach that the South African Athletics Board (SAAAB) ever had and I was the only manager that the SAAAB ever had. Wilfred did good work when it came to the general running of athletics. I served as treasurer of the SAAAB under the late Harry Hendricks.[15]

I made numerous changes to the management and organisation of athletics in the Western Cape. Courses were started for athletics officials, coaching and administration, of which Wilfred Daniels took the lead. These courses were run by qualified officials. Some of them went overseas to be qualified. At the end of the course there were exams that were written and the people who passed their exams were awarded certificates. This enabled us to have good officials to officiate at primary, high and senior level meetings. It was at these meetings that the Western Province teams were selected for track and field, cross-country and road running that participated at the South African Amateur Athletic Board Championships. In 1981 we established a headquarters at Vygieskraal Athletics Stadium.[16]

---

10 *Sun*, 23 June 1950, p. 8; *Sun*, 28 November 1952, p. 1.

11 A lecturer in physical education at the University of the Western Cape and a certified British Amateur Athletic Board coach, see Cleophas FJ 2018. *Creating a sport historian's life story*, p. 333.

12 Originally, a member of the Elsie's River Amateur Athletics club, Daniels, who is from Stellenbosch, helped establish the Stellenbosch Amateur Athletics Club in September 1976, see Du Plessis, C. 2017.

13 An athletics coach of the Spartans Amateur Athletic Club, see Eshmail, E. n.d.

14 A teacher at Steenberg High School in Cape Town and coach of Commonwealth Games athlete, Gavin Lendis and Olympians, Janice Josephs and Valentia da Rocha, *Southern Mail*. 1 June 2016, p. 24.

15 According to the dissertation of Paul Hendricks, "He contributed significantly to non-racial sport, as a founder member of the South African Senior Schools Sports Association (SASSSA), the South African Council on Sport (SACOS) and non-racial swimming. His eminent leadership qualities as a sports administrator, teacher, school principal and later rector of Bellville College of Education, meant he not only left an indellble mark on the educational landscape, but also the political movement in South Africa. Hendricks P. 2002. Engaging Apartheid: The Teachers' League of South Africa in the Western Cape, 1985–1989. Unpublished Masters thesis. Cape Town: University of Cape Town, p. 2.

16 A tartan athletic track in Athlone, Cape Town. The first of it's sort for Capetonian black athletes.

An annual programme was introduced by engaging athletic clubs to host athletic events with the assistance of the union. We became very successful with our athletic meetings because primary and high schools became involved at athletic meetings, with primary schools participating in the morning and then the senior schools, colleges and club athletes in the afternoons. This proved to be a great success and elevated athletics to the next level. Western Province Athletics (clubs), the high schools[17] and primary schools met on a regular basis for discussions and planning of our athletics. This eventually led to the colleges, primary and high schools having teams chosen to participate at the South African Amateur Athletics Board's Championships on a regular basis. We faced numerous challenges, lack of sponsorship, and we had to raise our own funds. Then, we only had one track, which was Vygieskraal. The windy conditions at Vygieskraal and other tracks resulted in athletes not really being able to perform at their best.

We started new clubs because the Group Areas Act forced many people to move from their areas and many clubs went defunct. We went into different areas and we encouraged people to start clubs in their areas. We went into Langa and Gugulethu where we started clubs. We went there without permits.[18] We also ran athletics meetings without fearing police intervention. They could be brutal when disrupting those meetings. Meetings of clubs were held at people's homes, in garages and under candlelight during those times. I went to visit many of these clubs and we had to sit in candlelight while having our meetings, but it worked well because people were really interested. Athletics meetings were held on a weekly basis at Vygieskraal, in Gugulethu, Langa and Bellville. We also travelled to Paarl and Worcester. The WPAAA had approximately sixteen affiliated clubs during the 1980s.

I remember the buses arriving two or three hours late for us to leave on tour. Buses broke down on the road and we had to sit for hours and wait for another bus to arrive, but we had good times. We had lots of fun on the road. When we arranged accommodation for athletes, they usually ended up staying at other athletes' houses as there was no money for hotels and guesthouses. We went to Natal with a big team. We hardly had any money but we could travel by air to the South African Amateur Athletic Track and Field meeting in Natal in 1975.

Politics

I was very controversial and outspoken. I was never afraid of authority, whether it was white, Coloured or black. I went to jail because I had protested at the Mike Gatting English Cricket Tour[19] match at Avendale Cricket Club at Clover Crescent, Athlone in 1989. The first person that they took that day was the president of the athletics, Harry Hendricks. All the leaders were arrested and loaded into big trucks and we eventually landed up at the Athlone police station. However, we had lots of support. People gathered outside that police station, hundreds of them, and we stayed for about a day.

Amateur Athletics had full membership of the SACOS but did not tie ourselves down to the rules and regulations that did not suit athletics. We made our own decisions with regards

---

[17] Cleophas FJ & Van der Merwe, FJG. 2009. *A historical overview of the Western Province Senior Schools Sports Union*, pp. 701–713.

[18] Non-residents of these African townships needed permits to enter them.

[19] The South African Cricket Union attempted to bypass international boycotts and successfully lured Mike Gatting to South Africa with a two-year contract for back-to-back cricket tours in the seasons of 1989–1990 and 1990–1991, Bacher A. 2004. *Ali. The life of Ali Bacher*. London: Penguin, p. 216.

to transgressions. I had a different outlook on transgressions.[20] I believe when people did something wrong during the Apartheid years, it was my duty and my union's duty to educate the athlete on what was expected. That was my belief.

We made our own decisions with regards to transgressions, and did not allow individuals to threaten us in any way. We followed the correct principles regarding no sport contact with our white counterparts. There were talks in the late 1980s that were held with the white athletics body, who wanted us to participate only in certain meetings. Our simple answer was that they either include everybody – primary school, high school, colleges – and we participate in all the meetings or nothing. We met with Jannie Momberg[21] in the late 1970s, and we also met at a later stage with Mike Walters, having talks and working together. Nothing materialised because they could not give us any guarantees that they were prepared to make sacrifice with us. They were not prepared to stand up against the government and its laws, therefore we were not prepared to work with them.

As head of Western Province Athletics I was very straightforward, pulling no punches, and was not afraid of anything or anybody. I did the right thing, not the good thing. I was sometimes not right in my approach but in the end athletics came first. Many of our administrators in the past had gone to jail because of their viewpoints and fighting for non-racialism in sport. We really only became, as sports people, aware of fighting the regime when SACOS was established in 1973.[22] I was a hardened SACOS man although I did not let SACOS dictate what we must do in athletics. We made our own decisions because we differed in many ways. In 1977, we appeared before SACOS because we used the UCT grounds in Pinelands. We went to the meeting, Herman Abrahams and myself, only the two of us. All those SACOS people sitting there. Colin Clarke was still the secretary then, he spoke the most. Colin, you have many tennis courts all over the show, and I named all the places, and then I said, *"Tell me Colin, where is there an athletics track?"* Silence, because we never had an athletics track, our athletic competitions were held on a grass track. If we wanted to use the Green Point Stadium we had to apply for a permit. That is why we did not use Green Point because of the permission that we had to apply for. We used Athlone Stadium, a pathetic grass track and not well looked after either. Eventually we got the use of Vygieskraal after a long fight with the Cape Town Council and that became our headquarters.

Apartheid caused many problems. It caused hatred: people could not fulfil their hopes, goals and dreams. There was mistrust amongst our own people because our own people were the people selling us out. There were limited choices of what you could become in life, there were misunderstandings amongst people and there was lack of development. I say here: no white person can put themselves in the shoes of a Coloured or black person.

We forever defied the law and organised events in Gugulethu and Langa without the required permits. Edwin Ngcawuzele, Mzoli (see photo) as we called him, played a very big role in our meetings at Langa and Guguletu. When travelling to venues outside the province

---

20 The SACOS had a Double Standards Resolution that forbade it's affliates' participation in any apartheid structure.

21 Initially, Momberg, a Stellenbosch farmer, was a National Party member. He joined the Democratic Party but later he became an African National Congress MP. He was vice-president of the SA Amateur Athletics Union. Known as "Jan Bek" for his loquaciousness.

22 The South African Council on Sport was established over the weekend of 17–18 March 1973 in the Verdic Hall in Durban with the purpose of establishing "a national body on non-racial lines", South African Council on Sport. 1973. Minutes of a General Meeting held at the Verdic Hall, 12 Carlisle Street, Durban, p. 4.

by bus, we defied the law. When we stopped in the Free State, we enjoyed visiting the shops when the sign said 'Whites only', we all walked into the shop together and I do not have to tell you what happened then.

Conclusion

In conclusion, although times have changed, very few good athletes are coming to the fore. In fact, the quality of athletics has declined, especially at school and club level. Whereas there was athletics and other extra-mural activities to keep children occupied and off the streets, now they are easily lured by drugs and gangs. With unity in the early nineties, the backstabbing began, with money becoming the root of all evil. During the unity talks, people were under the impression that we knew nothing about sport: we did not know how to run sport, we did not prepare things. However, they learnt differently. That was not the athletics I was accustomed to and I then decided to hang up my boots. For more than twenty years, I was involved in athletics and administration. I felt I had done my duty for my community and I feel fulfilled.

R. APRIL wins the open 880 yards event at the non-White Champion of Champions athletics at Green Point Track today

Robin April, the athlete
Source: Clement du Plessis, private collection

WESTERN PROVINCE ATHLETIC AND CYCLING ASSOCIATION
ESTABLISHED 1901
OFFICIALS 1972—73

Back Left to Right: H.D. Abrahams (Assistant), R.T. April (Joint Secretary), J. Vass (Trustee), C. Jacobs (Acting Secretary)
Front Left to Right: C. Jacobs (Treasurer), S.A. Hermansohn(?), J.R. Lentie (Chairman), R.A. van Rensie (Vice-Chairman), C. Plessis (Treasurer)

WPAACA executive in 1972
Source: Clement du Plessis, private collection

Edwin Ngcawuzele (Mzoli) and Robin April
at an athletics meeting in Langa in 1985
Source: Clement du Plessis, private collection

References

Bacher A. 2004. *Ali. The life of Ali Bacher*. London: Penguin.

Booley, A. *Forgotten heroes. History of Black rugby 1882–1992*. Cape Town: M. Booley.

Cape Herald, The. 1972. 16 September.

Cape Standard, The. 1939. 25 April.

Cleophas F.J. Creating a sport historian's life story narrative in society. *The International Journal of the History of Sport*. 2017. 34(5–6):330–334.

Cleophas F.J. & Van der Merwe, F.J.G. 2009. A historical overview of the Western Province Senior Schools Sports Union. 1956 to 1973. *African Journal for Physical, Health Education, Recreation and Dance (AJPHERD)*, December, 15(4):701–713.

Du Plessis, C. 2017, February. How Wilfred Daniels breathed new life into coaching [Selected stories online]. http://www.athleticsclipboard.co.za/athletics-news/how-wilfred-daniels-breathed-new-life-into-coaching/

Eshmail, E. n.d. Former athlete honours coach Willie Davids. http://www.athleticsclipboard.co.za/athletics-news/former-athlete-honours-coach-willie-davids/ [Retrieved 19 May 2018.]

Hendricks, P. 2002. Engaging Apartheid: The Teachers' League of South Africa in the Western Cape, 1985–1989. Unpublished Master's thesis. Cape Town: University of Cape Town.

Kloppers, W. 2018. Telephonic interview with former Hewat Training College athlete. 25 May.

South African Council on Sport. 1973. Minutes of a General Meeting held at the Verdic Hall, 12 Carlisle Street, Durban on Saturday 17 March.

Southern Mail. 2016. 1 June.

Sun, The. 1935. 3 May.

Sun, The. 1939. 3 March.

Sun, The. 1939. 28 April.

Sun, The. 1950. 23 June.

Sun, The. 1952. 28 November.

Western Province Cricket Board. 1982. Minutes of monthly council meeting held on Sunday 14 March 1982 in the Dahlia Restaurant, Malmesbury.